Official IELTS Practice Materials 2

Contents

A DVD containing the Practice Listening test and three sample candidate Speaking tests is included at the back of this booklet.

Introduction

These Practice Materials are intended to give IELTS candidates an idea of what the test is like. They also give candidates the opportunity to test themselves to see whether their English is at the level required to take IELTS.

Please note, however, that a high score on these Practice Materials does not guarantee that the same standard will be reached in the real IELTS test.

These Practice Materials are approved by the British Council, Cambridge ESOL and IDP: IELTS Australia.

Only those pages which carry the wording '© UCLES 2010 PHOTOCOPIABLE' may be copied.

Format of the IELTS Test

The IELTS test is made up of four components. All candidates take the same Listening and Speaking tests. There is a choice of Reading and Writing tests depending on whether you are an **ACADEMIC** or **GENERAL TRAINING** candidate.

The tests are normally taken in the order Listening, Reading, Writing, Speaking, and are timed as follows:

Listening	approximately 30 minutes
Reading	60 minutes
Writing	60 minutes
Speaking	11–14 minutes

Information on the test format can be found in *IELTS Information for Candidates*. This is available from test centres or can be downloaded from the IELTS website **www.ielts.org**

The website also contains further information on the test content, test administration and marking procedures.

How to Use the Practice Materials

Preparing to take the Practice Test

1 Decide which Reading and Writing tests you should take – **ACADEMIC** or **GENERAL TRAINING**.

The Academic module assesses the English language skills required for academic study or professional recognition.

The emphasis of the General Training module is on language skills in broad social and workplace contexts. It is suitable for candidates who are going to migrate to an English-speaking country (Australia, Canada, New Zealand, UK). It is also suitable for candidates planning to undertake work experience or training programmes not at degree level, or to complete their secondary education.

2 You need to write your answers on the answer sheets. The Listening/Reading answer sheets are on pages 82–83. Instructions on how to complete the Listening/Reading answer sheets are on page 81. The Writing answer booklet is on pages 84–87. You may photocopy the answer sheets/booklets so that they may be reused.

3 Prepare for the Practice Test carefully:

- Find a quiet room with a table to write on.

- Make sure that you are not going to be interrupted.

- Make sure that you have everything you need, i.e. pencils, pens, an eraser, a pencil sharpener and a computer with headphones, or a DVD player for the Listening test.

- Make sure you have a watch or clock. It is essential that you follow the time allowed for each component. There is a lot of material in the Reading and Writing tests and one of the aims of this Practice Test is to see how you can manage in the time allowed. **If you allow yourself longer than the test says, you will not get a true picture of your ability.**

Taking the Practice Test

1 Turn to the **Listening test** on page 5. Do not open it yet. Put the DVD in the DVD player/computer. Do not play it yet.

Read the instructions on the cover of the question paper and make sure you understand them. Start the Listening test (Full Test) on the DVD. Note that once you have started the DVD, you must not stop it. You must let it run straight through to the end. It will take about 30 minutes. You should write your answers as you listen in the spaces provided next to the questions on the question paper.

Once the recording has ended, do not listen to it again.

During the 10-minute pause at the end of the test, copy your answers carefully into the corresponding boxes on the answer sheet. For example, write the answer to question 1 in box 1.

2 Now turn to the appropriate **Reading test** (Academic or General Training) on pages 13 or 36. Read the instructions on the cover of the question paper and make sure you understand them. Make a note of the time and start the test.

You may write your answers directly on the answer sheet, or you may write your answers on the question paper and then copy them onto the answer sheet. Note, however, that no extra time is allowed for copying answers onto the answer sheet.

After 60 minutes, stop immediately.

3 Allow yourself a short break.

4 Now turn to the appropriate **Writing test** (Academic or General Training). There are three examples of the Academic Writing test on pages 27–35. There are two examples of the General Training Writing test on pages 49–54.

Read the instructions on the cover of the question paper. Once you are sure you understand them, make a note of the time and start the test.

Write your answers in the Writing answer booklet.

You should spend approximately 20 minutes on Task 1, and approximately 40 minutes on Task 2.

After 60 minutes, stop immediately.

5 Allow yourself a break.

6 There is information about the **Speaking test** and sample Speaking materials on pages 55–56.

Read through this material and practise making responses.

Marking the Practice Test

1 Read 'How to Mark the Listening and Reading Practice Tests' on page 57, and then check your answers to the Listening and Reading tests against those in the answer keys on page 58.

To interpret your Listening and Reading scores, read 'Interpreting your Scores' on page 62.

2 You cannot mark the Writing test yourself, but you will have a clearer idea of what is required in the time allowed. There is information on how Writing is assessed on page 63.

You will find sample answers to the Writing tasks on pages 64–78. Each answer has been given a Band Score and these are explained by examiner comments.

3 You cannot mark your speaking performance using the sample Speaking test materials, but there is information on how Speaking is assessed on page 79. On the DVD, there are three sample Speaking tests. On page 80, there are Band Scores and examiner comments for each sample candidate performance.

Taking the Practice Test again

1   If your scores on the Practice Test are low and you decide to have more English lessons or study to improve a language skill, you may want to take the test again to see if you have made progress before you apply to take IELTS. You should, therefore, put the Practice Materials away and not refer to them until you are ready to try again. If you do this, there is a good chance that you will have forgotten the answers and that the Practice Test will still give you a reasonable indication of the score you would get on IELTS. You should therefore not retake the Practice Test too soon after first taking it.

2   Please note that the Practice Materials are not designed to measure short-term progress. If you retake the Practice Test too soon, you may find that your scores are no higher than they were.

3   Once you have received a score you are satisfied with on the full Listening Practice Test, you may find it useful to listen to the separate sections (1–4) of the Listening Test on the DVD. However, you should only do this if you are sure you will not be retaking the full Listening Practice Test.

INTERNATIONAL ENGLISH LANGUAGE TESTING SYSTEM **0380/4**
0381/4

Listening

PRACTICE MATERIALS

Approximately 30 minutes

Additional materials:
    Answer sheet for Listening and Reading

Time   Approximately 30 minutes (plus 10 minutes' transfer time)

INSTRUCTIONS TO CANDIDATES

Do not open this question paper until you are told to do so.

Write your name and candidate number in the spaces at the top of this page.

Listen to the instructions for each part of the paper carefully.

Answer all the questions.

While you are listening, write your answers on the question paper.

You will have 10 minutes at the end of the test to copy your answers onto the separate answer sheet. Use a pencil.

At the end of the test, hand in this question paper.

INFORMATION FOR CANDIDATES

There are **four** parts to the test.

You will hear each part **once** only.

There are **40** questions.

Each question carries one mark.

For each part of the test, there will be time for you to look through the questions and time for you to check your answers.

SECTION 1   Questions 1 – 10

Complete the form below.

*Write **ONE WORD AND/OR A NUMBER** for each answer.*

THEATRE ROYAL PLYMOUTH Booking Form	
Example Performance:	*The ....**Impostor**.........*
Date:	*Saturday* **1** ....
Time:	**2** ....
Tickets:	*three adults and one child*
Seats in:	*the* **3** ....
Seat row/number(s):	**4** ....
Method of delivery:	*post*
Total payment:	*£39*
Card details:	
Type:	**5** ....
Number:	**6** ....
Name:	*Mr J.* **7** ....
Address:	**8** .... *Street,* *London* **9** ....
Additional requests:	*put on the mailing list* *book* **10** ....

SECTION 2

Questions 11 – 20

Questions 11 – 17

Label the plan of the rock festival site below.

*Choose **SEVEN** answers from the box and write the correct letter, **A-I**, next to questions 11-17.*

A   art exhibition
B   band entrance
C   car park
D   craft fair
E   exhibitors' entrance
F   fringe stage
G   lock-up garages
H   main stage
I   restaurant

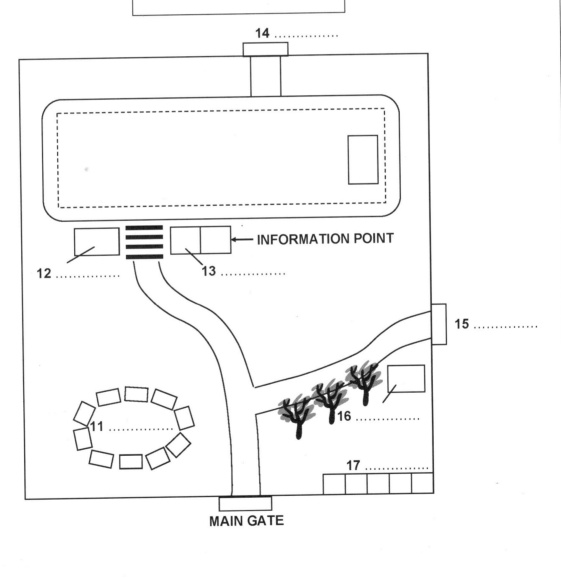

14 ....

INFORMATION POINT

12 ....

13 ....

15 ....

16 ....

11 ....

17 ....

MAIN GATE

Turn over ▶

Questions 18 – 20

Complete the sentences below.

*Write **NO MORE THAN TWO WORDS** for each answer.*

18   To show you are an official visitor, you have to wear the .... provided.

19   Cars blocking paths could prevent access by .... in an emergency.

20   To reclaim items from storage, you must show your ....

SECTION 3   *Questions 21 – 30*

Questions 21 – 23

*Choose **THREE** letters, **A-G**.*

Which **THREE** factors does Marco's tutor advise him to consider when selecting a course?

     A   possibility of specialisation
     B   relevance to future career
     C   personal interest
     D   organisation of course
     E   assessment methods
     F   range of topics
     G   reputation of lecturer

Questions 24 – 27

*Choose the correct letter, **A**, **B** or **C**.*

24   Why does Marco's tutor advise him to avoid the *Team Management* course?

     A   It will repeat work that Marco has already done.
     B   It is intended for students at a lower level than Marco.
     C   It may take too much time to do well.

25   Why does Marco want to do a dissertation?

     A   He thinks it will help his future career.
     B   He would like to do a detailed study.
     C   He has already done some work for it.

26   What does Marco's tutor think about the dissertation outline?

     A   The topic is too narrow to be useful.
     B   The available data may be unsuitable.
     C   The research plan is too complicated.

27   What does Marco decide to do about his dissertation?

     A   contact potential interviewees
     B   change to another topic
     C   discuss it with Professor Briggs

Turn over ▶

Questions 28 – 30

Complete the sentences below.

*Write **NO MORE THAN TWO WORDS** for each answer.*

Practical details

28   A first draft of the dissertation should be completed by the end of ....

29   The dissertation should be registered with the .... of the department.

30   Marco should get a copy of the statistics software from the ....

SECTION 4   *Questions 31 – 40*

Questions 31 – 33

Complete the notes below.

*Write **ONE WORD ONLY** for each answer.*

The Tiger Shark

- **Origin of name:** its dark bands

- **Size:** 6.5 metres (maximum)

- **Preferred habitat:** near to the **31** ....

- **Typical food:** other sea creatures but also **32** .... produced by humans

- **Raine Island area:** studies show tiger sharks are mainly found here during the **33** .... (when turtles are nesting)

Questions 34 – 38

Complete the flow-chart below.

*Write **ONE WORD ONLY** for each answer.*

Shark Tagging Process

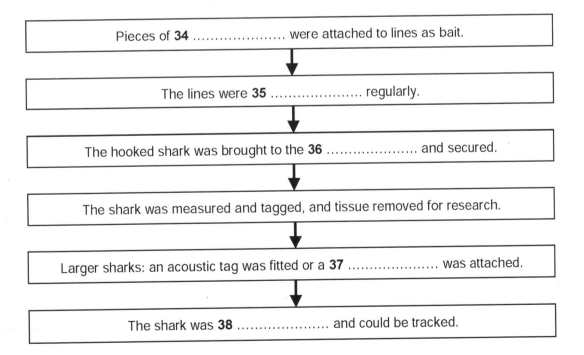

Pieces of **34** .... were attached to lines as bait.

↓

The lines were **35** .... regularly.

↓

The hooked shark was brought to the **36** .... and secured.

↓

The shark was measured and tagged, and tissue removed for research.

↓

Larger sharks: an acoustic tag was fitted or a **37** .... was attached.

↓

The shark was **38** .... and could be tracked.

Turn over ▶

Questions 39 and 40

Choose the correct letter, A, B or C.

39 The purpose of the research was to understand the tiger sharks'

    A reproductive patterns.
    B migration patterns.
    C feeding patterns.

40 Observations showed that, in general, tiger sharks

    A change depths frequently.
    B usually avoid the surface of the water.
    C often spend long periods on the ocean floor.

Candidate Number

Candidate Name

INTERNATIONAL ENGLISH LANGUAGE TESTING SYSTEM   0381/1

Academic Reading

PRACTICE MATERIALS   1 hour

Additional materials:
     Answer sheet for Listening and Reading

Time   1 hour

INSTRUCTIONS TO CANDIDATES

Do not open this question paper until you are told to do so.

Write your name and candidate number in the spaces at the top of this page.

Read the instructions for each part of the paper carefully.

Answer all the questions.

Write your answers on the answer sheet. Use a pencil.

You **must** complete the answer sheet within the time limit.

At the end of the test, hand in both this question paper and your answer sheet.

INFORMATION FOR CANDIDATES

There are **40** questions on this question paper.

Each question carries one mark.

PV1

© UCLES 2010

READING PASSAGE 1

You should spend about 20 minutes on **Questions 1-13**, which are based on Reading Passage 1 on pages 3 and 4.

Questions 1 – 6

Reading Passage 1 has six paragraphs, **A-F**.

Choose the correct heading for each paragraph from the list of headings below.

Write the correct number, **i-ix**, in boxes 1-6 on your answer sheet.

List of Headings
i   The appearance and location of different seaweeds
ii   The nutritional value of seaweeds
iii   How seaweeds reproduce and grow
iv   How to make agar from seaweeds
v   The under-use of native seaweeds
vi   Seaweed species at risk of extinction
vii   Recipes for how to cook seaweeds
viii   The range of seaweed products
ix   Why seaweeds don't sink or dry out

1   Paragraph **A**

2   Paragraph **B**

3   Paragraph **C**

4   Paragraph **D**

5   Paragraph **E**

6   Paragraph **F**

Seaweeds of New Zealand

A   Seaweed is a particularly wholesome food, which absorbs and concentrates traces of a wide variety of minerals necessary to the body's health. Many elements may occur in seaweed – aluminium, barium, calcium, chlorine, copper, iodine and iron, to name but a few – traces normally produced by erosion and carried to the seaweed beds by river and sea currents. Seaweeds are also rich in vitamins; indeed, Inuits obtain a high proportion of their bodily requirements of vitamin C from the seaweeds they eat. The health benefits of seaweed have long been recognised. For instance, there is a remarkably low incidence of goitre among the Japanese, and also among New Zealand's indigenous Maori people, who have always eaten seaweeds, and this may well be attributed to the high iodine content of this food. Research into historical Maori eating customs shows that jellies were made using seaweeds, nuts, fuchsia and tutu berries, cape gooseberries, and many other fruits both native to New Zealand and sown there from seeds brought by settlers and explorers. As with any plant life, some seaweeds are more palatable than others, but in a survival situation, most seaweeds could be chewed to provide a certain sustenance.

B   New Zealand lays claim to approximately 700 species of seaweed, some of which have no representation outside that country. Of several species grown worldwide, New Zealand also has a particularly large share. For example, it is estimated that New Zealand has some 30 species of *Gigartina*, a close relative of carrageen or Irish moss. These are often referred to as the New Zealand carrageens. The substance called agar which can be extracted from these species gives them great commercial application in the production of seameal, from which seameal custard (a food product) is made, and in the canning, paint and leather industries. Agar is also used in the manufacture of cough mixtures, cosmetics, confectionery and toothpastes. In fact, during World War II, New Zealand *Gigartina* were sent to Australia to be used in toothpaste.

C   New Zealand has many of the commercially profitable red seaweeds, several species of which are a source of agar (*Pterocladia, Gelidium, Chondrus, Gigartina*). Despite this, these seaweeds were not much utilised until several decades ago. Although distribution of the *Gigartina* is confined to certain areas according to species, it is only on the east coast of the North Island that its occurrence is rare. And even then, the east coast, and the area around Hokianga, have a considerable supply of the two species of *Pterocladia* from which agar is also made. New Zealand used to import the Northern Hemisphere Irish moss (*Chondrus crispus*) from England and ready-made agar from Japan.

Turn over ▶

D   Seaweeds are divided into three classes determined by colour – red, brown and green – and each tends to live in a specific position. However, except for the unmistakable sea lettuce (*Ulva*), few are totally one colour; and especially when dry, some species can change colour significantly – a brown one may turn quite black, or a red one appear black, brown, pink or purple. Identification is nevertheless facilitated by the fact that the factors which determine where a seaweed will grow are quite precise, and they tend therefore to occur in very well-defined zones. Although there are exceptions, the green seaweeds are mainly shallow-water algae; the browns belong to the medium depths; and the reds are plants of the deeper water, furthest from the shore. Those shallow-water species able to resist long periods of exposure to sun and air are usually found on the upper shore, while those less able to withstand such exposure occur nearer to, or below, the low-water mark. Radiation from the sun, the temperature level, and the length of time immersed also play a part in the zoning of seaweeds. Flat rock surfaces near mid-level tides are the most usual habitat of sea-bombs, Venus' necklace, and most brown seaweeds. This is also the home of the purple laver or Maori *karengo*, which looks rather like a reddish-purple lettuce. Deep-water rocks on open coasts, exposed only at very low tide, are usually the site of bull-kelp, strapweeds and similar tough specimens. Kelp, or bladder kelp, has stems that rise to the surface from massive bases or 'holdfasts', the leafy branches and long ribbons of leaves surging with the swells beyond the line of shallow coastal breakers or covering vast areas of calmer coastal water.

E   Propagation of seaweeds occurs by seed-like spores, or by fertilisation of egg cells. None have roots in the usual sense; few have leaves; and none have flowers, fruits or seeds. The plants absorb their nourishment through their leafy fronds when they are surrounded by water; the holdfast of seaweeds is purely an attaching organ, not an absorbing one.

F   Some of the large seaweeds stay on the surface of the water by means of air-filled floats; others, such as bull-kelp, have large cells filled with air. Some which spend a good part of their time exposed to the air, often reduce dehydration either by having swollen stems that contain water, or they may (like Venus' necklace) have swollen nodules, or they may have a distinctive shape like a sea-bomb. Others, like the sea cactus, are filled with a slimy fluid or have a coating of mucilage on the surface. In some of the larger kelps, this coating is not only to keep the plant moist, but also to protect it from the violent action of waves.

Questions 7 – 10

Complete the flow-chart below.

Choose **NO MORE THAN THREE WORDS** from the passage for each answer.

Write your answers in boxes 7-10 on your answer sheet.

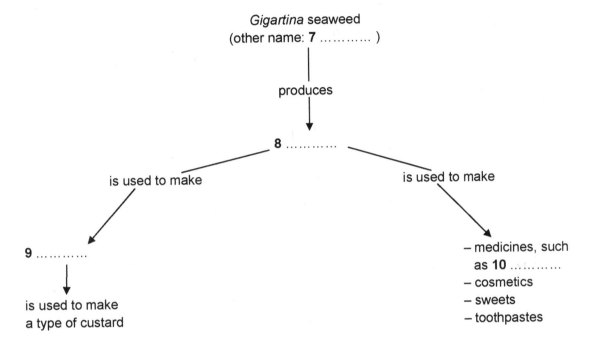

Gigartina seaweed
(other name: **7** ....)

↓

produces

↓

8 ....

is used to make   is used to make

9 ....   – medicines, such
                                                  as **10** ....
↓   – cosmetics
                                                  – sweets
is used to make   – toothpastes
a type of custard

Questions 11 – 13

Classify the following characteristics as belonging to

    A   brown seaweed
    B   green seaweed
    C   red seaweed

Write the correct letter, **A**, **B** or **C**, in boxes 11-13 on your answer sheet.

11   can survive the heat and dryness at the high-water mark

12   grow far out in the open sea

13   share their site with *karengo* seaweed

Turn over ▶

READING PASSAGE 2

*You should spend about 20 minutes on **Questions 14-26**, which are based on Reading Passage 2 on pages 6 and 7.*

TWO WINGS AND A TOOLKIT

A research team at Oxford University discover the remarkable toolmaking skills of New Caledonian crows

Betty and her mate Abel are captive crows in the care of Alex Kacelnik, an expert in animal behaviour at Oxford University. They belong to a forest-dwelling species of bird (*Corvus moneduloides*) confined to two islands in the South Pacific. New Caledonian crows are tenacious predators, and the only birds that habitually use a wide selection of self-made tools to find food.

One of the wild crows' cleverest tools is the crochet hook, made by detaching a side twig from a larger one, leaving enough of the larger twig to shape into a hook. Equally cunning is a tool crafted from the barbed vine-leaf, which consists of a central rib with paired leaflets each with a rose-like thorn at its base. They strip out a piece of this rib, removing the leaflets and all but one thorn at the top, which remains as a ready-made hook to prise out insects from awkward cracks.

The crows also make an ingenious tool called a padanus probe from padanus tree leaves. The tool has a broad base, sharp tip, a row of tiny hooks along one edge, and a tapered shape created by the crow nipping and tearing to form a progression of three or four steps along the other edge of the leaf. What makes this tool special is that they manufacture it to a standard design, as if following a set of instructions. Although it is rare to catch a crow in the act of clipping out a padanus probe, we do have ample proof of their workmanship: the discarded leaves from which the tools are cut. The remarkable thing that these 'counterpart' leaves tell us is that crows consistently produce the same design every time, with no in-between or trial versions. It's left the researchers wondering whether, like people, they envisage the tool before they start and perform the actions they know are needed to make it. Research has revealed that genetics plays a part in the less sophisticated toolmaking skills of finches in the Galápagos islands. No one knows if that's also the case for New Caledonian crows, but it's highly unlikely that their toolmaking skills are hardwired into the brain. 'The picture so far points to a combination of cultural transmission – from parent birds to their young – and individual resourcefulness,' says Kacelnik.

In a test at Oxford, Kacelnik's team offered Betty and Abel an original challenge – food in a bucket at the bottom of a 'well'. The only way to get the food was to hook the bucket out by its handle. Given a choice of tools – a straight length of wire and one with a hooked end – the birds immediately picked the hook, showing that they did indeed understand the functional properties of the tool.

But do they also have the foresight and creativity to plan the construction of their tools? It appears they do. In one bucket-in-the-well test, Abel carried off the hook, leaving Betty with nothing but the straight wire. 'What happened next was absolutely amazing,' says Kacelnik. She wedged the tip of the wire into a crack in a plastic dish and pulled the other end to fashion her own hook. Wild crows don't have access to pliable, bendable material that retains its shape, and Betty's only similar experience was a brief encounter with some pipe cleaners a year earlier. In nine out of ten further tests, she again made hooks and retrieved the bucket.

The question of what's going on in a crow's mind will take time and a lot more experiments to answer, but there could be a lesson in it for understanding our own evolution. Maybe our ancestors, who suddenly began to create symmetrical tools with carefully worked edges some 1.5 million years ago, didn't actually have the sophisticated mental abilities with which we credit them. Closer scrutiny of the brains of New Caledonian crows might provide a few pointers to the special attributes they would have needed. 'If we're lucky we may find specific developments in the brain that set these animals apart,' says Kacelnik.

One of these might be a very strong degree of laterality – the specialisation of one side of the brain to perform specific tasks. In people, the left side of the brain controls the processing of complex sequential tasks, and also language and speech. One of the consequences of this is thought to be right-handedness. Interestingly, biologists have noticed that most padanus probes are cut from the left side of the leaf, meaning that the birds clip them with the right side of their beaks – the crow equivalent of right-handedness. The team thinks this reflects the fact that the left side of the crow's brain is specialised to handle the sequential processing required to make complex tools.

Under what conditions might this extraordinary talent have emerged in these two species? They are both social creatures, and wide-ranging in their feeding habits. These factors were probably important but, ironically, it may have been their shortcomings that triggered the evolution of toolmaking. Maybe the ancestors of crows and humans found themselves in a position where they couldn't make the physical adaptations required for survival – so they had to change their behaviour instead. The stage was then set for the evolution of those rare cognitive skills that produce sophisticated tools. New Caledonian crows may tell us what those crucial skills are.

Turn over ▶

Questions 14 – 17

Label the diagrams below.

*Choose **NO MORE THAN TWO WORDS** from the passage for each answer.*

Write your answers in boxes 14-17 on your answer sheet.

THREE TOOLS MADE BY CROWS

<u>**a)**</u>   **14** ....

remains of larger twig

side twig

<u>**b)**   Barbed vine-leaf stick</u>

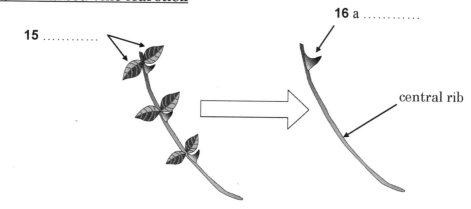

15 ....

16 a ....

central rib

<u>**c)**   Padanus probe</u>

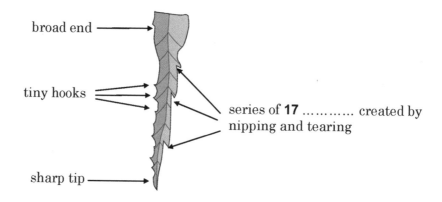

broad end

tiny hooks

series of **17** .... created by nipping and tearing

sharp tip

Questions 18 – 23

Do the following statements agree with the information given in Reading Passage 2?

In boxes 18-23 on your answer sheet, write

TRUE	*if the statement agrees with the information*
FALSE	*if the statement contradicts the information*
NOT GIVEN	*if there is no information on this*

18   There appears to be a fixed pattern for the padanus probe's construction.

19   There is plenty of evidence to indicate how the crows manufacture the padanus probe.

20   Crows seem to practise a number of times before making a usable padanus probe.

21   The researchers suspect the crows have a mental image of the padanus probe before they create it.

22   Research into how the padanus probe is made has helped to explain the toolmaking skills of many other bird species.

23   The researchers believe the ability to make the padanus probe is passed down to the crows in their genes.

Questions 24 – 26

Choose **THREE** letters, **A-G**.

Write the correct letters in boxes 24-26 on your answer sheet.

According to the information in the passage, which **THREE** of the following features are probably common to both New Caledonian crows and human beings?

A	keeping the same mate for life
B	having few natural predators
C	having a bias to the right when working
D	being able to process sequential tasks
E	living in extended family groups
F	eating a variety of foodstuffs
G	being able to adapt to diverse habitats

Turn over ▶

READING PASSAGE 3

*You should spend about 20 minutes on **Questions 27-40**, which are based on Reading Passage 3 on pages 10 and 11.*

How did writing begin?

Many theories, few answers

The Sumerians, an ancient people of the Middle East, had a story explaining the invention of writing more than 5,000 years ago. It seems a messenger of the King of Uruk arrived at the court of a distant ruler so exhausted that he was unable to deliver the oral message. So the king set down the words of his next messages on a clay tablet. A charming story, whose retelling at a recent symposium at the University of Pennsylvania amused scholars. They smiled at the absurdity of a letter which the recipient would not have been able to read. They also doubted that the earliest writing was a direct rendering of speech. Writing more likely began as a separate, symbolic system of communication and only later merged with spoken language.

Yet in the story the Sumerians, who lived in Mesopotamia, in what is now southern Iraq, seemed to understand writing's transforming function. As Dr Holly Pittman, director of the University's Center for Ancient Studies, observed, writing 'arose out of the need to store and transmit information ... over time and space'.

In exchanging interpretations and information, the scholars acknowledged that they still had no fully satisfying answers to the questions of how and why writing developed. Many favoured an explanation of writing's origins in the visual arts, pictures becoming increasingly abstract and eventually representing spoken words. Their views clashed with a widely held theory among archaeologists that writing developed from the pieces of clay that Sumerian accountants used as tokens to keep track of goods.

Archaeologists generally concede that they have no definitive answer to the question of whether writing was invented only once, or arose independently in several places, such as Egypt, the Indus Valley, China, Mexico and Central America. The preponderance of archaeological data shows that the urbanizing Sumerians were the first to develop writing, in 3,200 or 3,300 BC. These are the dates for many clay tablets in an early form of cuneiform, a script written by pressing the end of a sharpened stick into wet clay, found at the site of the ancient city of Uruk. The baked clay tablets bore such images as pictorial symbols of the names of people, places and things connected with government and commerce. The Sumerian script gradually evolved from the pictorial to the abstract, but did not at first represent recorded spoken language.

Cuneiform Writing

Dr Peter Damerow, a specialist in Sumerian cuneiform at the Max Planck Institute for the History of Science in Berlin, said, 'It is likely that there were mutual influences of writing systems around the world. However, their great variety now shows that the development of writing, once initiated, attains a considerable degree of independence and flexibility to adapt to specific characteristics of the sounds of the language to be represented.' Not that he accepts the conventional view that writing started as a representation of words by pictures. New studies of early Sumerian writing, he said, challenge this interpretation. The structures of this earliest writing did not, for example, match the structure of spoken language, dealing mainly in lists and categories rather than in sentences and narrative.

For at least two decades, Dr Denise Schmandt-Besserat, a University of Texas archaeologist, has argued that the first writing grew directly out of a system practised by Sumerian accountants. They used clay tokens, each one shaped to represent a jar of oil, a container of grain or a particular kind of livestock. These tokens were sealed inside clay spheres, and then the number and type of tokens inside was recorded on the outside using impressions resembling the tokens. Eventually, the token impressions were replaced with inscribed signs, and writing had been invented.

Though Dr Schmandt-Besserat has won much support, some linguists question her thesis, and others, like Dr Pittman, think it too narrow. They emphasise that pictorial representation and writing evolved together. 'There's no question that the token system is a forerunner of writing,' Dr Pittman said, 'but I have an argument with her evidence for a link between tokens and signs, and she doesn't open up the process to include picture making.'

Dr Schmandt-Besserat vigorously defended her ideas. 'My colleagues say that pictures were the beginning of writing,' she said, 'but show me a single picture that becomes a sign in writing. They say that designs on pottery were the beginning of writing, but show me a single sign of writing you can trace back to a pot – it doesn't exist.' In its first 500 years, she asserted, cuneiform writing was used almost solely for recording economic information, and after that its uses multiplied and broadened.

Yet other scholars have advanced different ideas. Dr Piotr Michalowski, Professor of Near East Civilizations at the University of Michigan, said that the proto-writing of Sumerian Uruk was 'so radically different as to be a complete break with the past'. It no doubt served, he said, to store and communicate information, but also became a new instrument of power. Some scholars noted that the origins of writing may not always have been in economics. In Egypt, most early writing is high on monuments or deep in tombs. In this case, said Dr Pascal Vernus from a university in Paris, early writing was less administrative than sacred. It seems that the only certainty in this field is that many questions remain to be answered.

Turn over ▶

Questions 27 – 30

Choose the correct letter, **A, B, C or D**.

Write the correct letter in boxes 27-30 on your answer sheet.

27   The researchers at the symposium regarded the story of the King of Uruk as ridiculous because

    A   writing probably developed independently of speech.
    B   clay tablets had not been invented at that time.
    C   the distant ruler would have spoken another language.
    D   evidence of writing has been discovered from an earlier period.

28   According to the writer, the story of the King of Uruk

    A   is a probable explanation of the origins of writing.
    B   proves that early writing had a different function to writing today.
    C   provides an example of symbolic writing.
    D   shows some awareness amongst Sumerians of the purpose of writing.

29   There was disagreement among the researchers at the symposium about

    A   the area where writing began.
    B   the nature of early writing materials.
    C   the way writing began.
    D   the meaning of certain abstract images.

30   The opponents of the theory that writing developed from tokens believe that it

    A   grew out of accountancy.
    B   evolved from pictures.
    C   was initially intended as decoration.
    D   was unlikely to have been connected with commerce.

Questions 31 – 36

Look at the following statements (Questions 31-36) and the list of people below.

*Match each statement with the correct person, **A-E**.*

*Write the correct letter, **A-E**, in boxes 31-36 on your answer sheet.*

NB *You may use any letter more than once.*

31   There is no proof that early writing is connected to decorated household objects.

32   As writing developed, it came to represent speech.

33   Sumerian writing developed into a means of political control.

34   Early writing did not represent the grammatical features of speech.

35   There is no convincing proof that tokens and signs are connected.

36   The uses of cuneiform writing were narrow at first, and later widened.

List of People

A   Dr Holly Pittman
B   Dr Peter Damerow
C   Dr Denise Schmandt-Besserat
D   Dr Piotr Michalowski
E   Dr Pascal Vernus

Turn over ▶

Questions 37 – 40

*Complete the summary using the list of words, **A-N**, below.*

*Write the correct letter, **A-N**, in boxes 37-40 on your answer sheet.*

The earliest form of writing

Most archaeological evidence shows that the people of **37** .... invented writing in around 3,300 BC. Their script was written on **38** .... and was called **39** .... Their script originally showed images related to political power and business, and later developed to become more **40** ....

A	cuneiform	B	pictorial	C	tomb walls
D	urban	E	legible	F	stone blocks
G	simple	H	Mesopotamia	I	abstract
J	papyrus sheets	K	decorative	L	clay tablets
M	Egypt	N	Uruk		

INTERNATIONAL ENGLISH LANGUAGE TESTING SYSTEM **0381/2**

Academic Writing

PRACTICE MATERIALS   **Example 1**   1 hour

Additional materials:
    Writing answer booklet

Time   1 hour

INSTRUCTIONS TO CANDIDATES

Do not open this question paper until you are told to do so.

Write your name and candidate number in the spaces at the top of this page.

Read the instructions for each task carefully.

Answer both of the tasks.

Write at least 150 words for Task 1.

Write at least 250 words for Task 2.

Write your answers in the answer booklet.

Write clearly in pen or pencil. You may make alterations, but make sure your work is easy to read.

At the end of the test, hand in both this question paper and your answer booklet.

INFORMATION FOR CANDIDATES

There are **two** tasks on this question paper.

Task 2 contributes twice as much as Task 1 to the Writing score.

WRITING TASK 1

You should spend about 20 minutes on this task.

The charts below show the proportions of the world's oil resources held in different areas, together with the proportions consumed annually in the same areas.

Summarise the information by selecting and reporting the main features, and make comparisons where relevant.

Write at least 150 words.

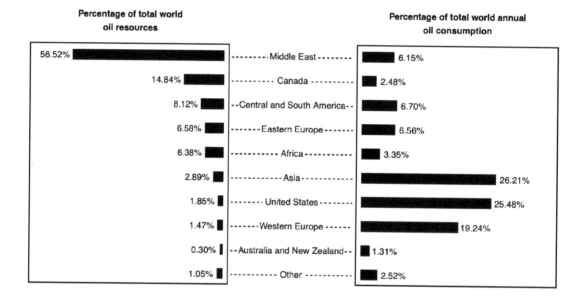

WRITING TASK 2

You should spend about 40 minutes on this task.

Write about the following topic:

> *In many countries today insufficient respect is shown to older people.*
>
> *What do you think may be the reasons for this?*
>
> *What problems might this cause in society?*

Give reasons for your answer and include any relevant examples from your own knowledge or experience.

Write at least 250 words.

INTERNATIONAL ENGLISH LANGUAGE TESTING SYSTEM **0381/2**

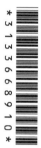

Academic Writing

PRACTICE MATERIALS   **Example 2**   1 hour

Additional materials:
   Writing answer booklet

Time   1 hour

INSTRUCTIONS TO CANDIDATES

Do not open this question paper until you are told to do so.

Write your name and candidate number in the spaces at the top of this page.

Read the instructions for each task carefully.

Answer both of the tasks.

Write at least 150 words for Task 1.

Write at least 250 words for Task 2.

Write your answers in the answer booklet.

Write clearly in pen or pencil. You may make alterations, but make sure your work is easy to read.

At the end of the test, hand in both this question paper and your answer booklet.

INFORMATION FOR CANDIDATES

There are **two** tasks on this question paper.

Task 2 contributes twice as much as Task 1 to the Writing score.

© UCLES 2010

WRITING TASK 1

You should spend about 20 minutes on this task.

The diagrams below show the site of a school in 2004 and the plan for changes to the school site in 2024.

Summarise the information by selecting and reporting the main features, and make comparisons where relevant.

Write at least 150 words.

School Site - 2004: 600 students

School Site - 2024: 1,000 students

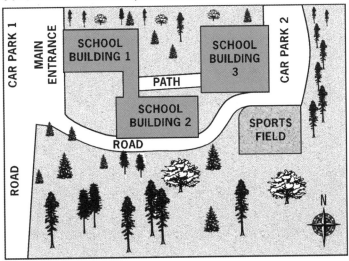

WRITING TASK 2

You should spend about 40 minutes on this task.

Write about the following topic:

It is important to ensure that children with a wide range of abilities and from a variety of social backgrounds mix with each other at school.

To what extent do you agree or disagree?

Give reasons for your answer and include any relevant examples from your own knowledge or experience.

Write at least 250 words.

INTERNATIONAL ENGLISH LANGUAGE TESTING SYSTEM 0381/2

Academic Writing

PRACTICE MATERIALS   **Example 3**   1 hour

Additional materials:
   Writing answer booklet

Time   1 hour

INSTRUCTIONS TO CANDIDATES

Do not open this question paper until you are told to do so.

Write your name and candidate number in the spaces at the top of this page.

Read the instructions for each task carefully.

Answer both of the tasks.

Write at least 150 words for Task 1.

Write at least 250 words for Task 2.

Write your answers in the answer booklet.

Write clearly in pen or pencil. You may make alterations, but make sure your work is easy to read.

At the end of the test, hand in both this question paper and your answer booklet.

INFORMATION FOR CANDIDATES

There are **two** tasks on this question paper.

Task 2 contributes twice as much as Task 1 to the Writing score.

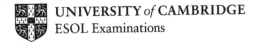

© UCLES 2010

WRITING TASK 1

You should spend about 20 minutes on this task.

The pie charts below show how dangerous waste products are dealt with in three countries.

Summarise the information by selecting and reporting the main features, and make comparisons where relevant.

Write at least 150 words.

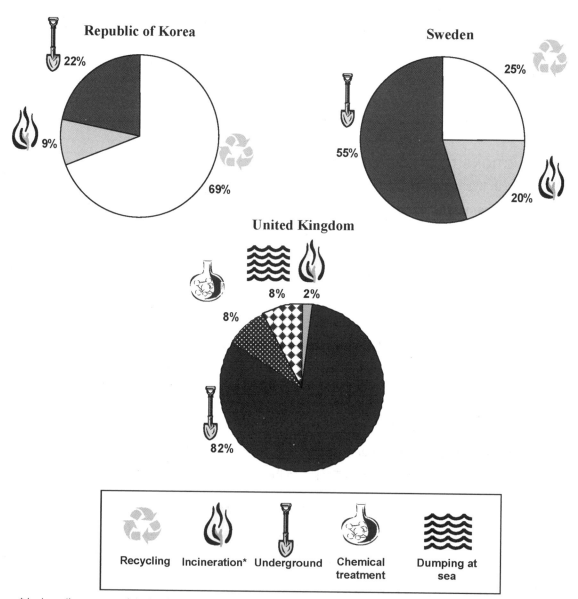

* Incineration: a way of destroying something by fire

WRITING TASK 2

You should spend about 40 minutes on this task.

Write about the following topic:

> *Some people think that strict punishments for driving offences are the key to reducing traffic accidents. Others, however, believe that other measures would be more effective in improving road safety.*
>
> *Discuss both these views and give your own opinion.*

Give reasons for your answer and include any relevant examples from your own knowledge or experience.

Write at least 250 words.

INTERNATIONAL ENGLISH LANGUAGE TESTING SYSTEM   **0380/1**

General Training Reading

PRACTICE MATERIALS   1 hour

Additional materials:
    Answer sheet for Listening and Reading

Time   1 hour

INSTRUCTIONS TO CANDIDATES

Do not open this question paper until you are told to do so.

Write your name and candidate number in the spaces at the top of this page.

Read the instructions for each part of the paper carefully.

Answer all the questions.

Write your answers on the answer sheet. Use a pencil.

You **must** complete the answer sheet within the time limit.

At the end of the test, hand in both this question paper and your answer sheet.

INFORMATION FOR CANDIDATES

There are **40** questions on this question paper.

Each question carries one mark.

PV1

© UCLES 2010

SECTION 1   Questions 1 – 14

Read the text below and answer Questions 1-8.

Visit these historic houses in Northern Ireland!

Ardress House

House tours of this elegant 17th-century farmhouse include the impressive drawing-room, fine furniture and paintings. The farmyard, complete with traditional farm implements, is very popular with children. A new programme of family events is arranged each year.

The Argory

This handsome 1820 house has remained unchanged since 1900. It demonstrates the decorative taste of the family who lived here at that time, and also includes a barrel organ that plays traditional Irish tunes once a month during house tours. There are horse carriages, a harness room, and a laundry in the imposing stable yard. As the house has no electric light, visitors wishing to make a close study of the interior and paintings should avoid dull days early and late in the season.

Castle Coole

Castle Coole is one of the finest late 18th-century houses in Ireland. The guided tour shows the rich interior decoration, furnishings and furniture of the time, the state bedroom prepared for the visit of King George IV in 1821, and the elegant hall, where evening concerts of classical music are often held.

Castle Ward

This mid-18th-century mansion is an architectural oddity of its time, the inside and outside having been built in two distinct architectural styles. In the surrounding estate there are many holiday cottages available for private lets as well as a caravan site.

Hezlett House

One of the few buildings in Northern Ireland surviving from before the 18th century, this 17th-century thatched house is simply furnished in late 19th-century style. There is a small museum of farm implements. There are picnic tables outside the house, and for younger visitors a landscaped play area is provided.

Springhill

An atmospheric 17th-century home, in a most attractive setting. The house tour takes in the exceptional library, family furniture from the 19th century, the nursery, and the unusual and colourful exhibition of costumes, which has some fine 17th-century Irish pieces.

Questions 1 – 8

Look at the following statements (Questions 1-8) and the list of houses below.

*Match each statement with the correct house, **A-F**.*

*Write the correct letter, **A-F**, in boxes 1-8 on your answer sheet.*

NB   *You may use any letter more than once.*

1   This house contains furniture of the period when it was built.

2   This building is described as having an unusual appearance.

3   Clothes from the past can be seen here.

4   Children are permitted to play games here.

5   A musical instrument exhibited here can sometimes be heard.

6   Parents can take part in the same activities as their children.

7   Accommodation is available in the grounds of the house.

8   Visibility indoors depends on the weather conditions.

> **List of Houses**
>
> A   Ardress House
> B   The Argory
> C   Castle Coole
> D   Castle Ward
> E   Hezlett House
> F   Springhill

Turn over ▶

Read the text below and answer Questions 9-14.

ANGLIAN WATER

This leaflet sets out our service pledges, with details on special care and new facilities for customers. We have other leaflets giving you further information on some subjects. Let us know which ones you would like by completing and posting the reply-paid section at the back of this leaflet.

We are committed to giving you the best customer service.

This means:

Being easy to contact
We have a freephone number for billing matters and a local charge 24-hour number for any service queries.

Keeping appointments
For written appointments, we will specify morning or afternoon to suit you (but cannot guarantee a precise time). If we have to change the arrangement, we will give you 24 hours' notice.

Answering your letters promptly
Within 10 working days for a complaint about water or sewerage services and within 20 working days if you have a billing query. If we can, we'll get back to you sooner.

No-quibble compensation if we get it wrong
We will pay £10 compensation if we fail to meet any of our guaranteed standards.

We care for every customer but we recognise that there are some who need that bit of extra help.

For our elderly or disabled customers we have a range of additional services, including your bill in Braille, help with reading your meter, or special care if for any reason you lose your water supply.

If English is not your first language and you need help understanding your bill, Language Line is a confidential telephone service which gives you information in your own language, at no extra cost.

Ring our freephone number (0800-919155) and ask for Language Line. Please tell us which language you need.

Questions 9 – 14

Do the following statements agree with the information given in the text on page 4?

In boxes 9-14 on your answer sheet, write

TRUE	*if the statement agrees with the information*
FALSE	*if the statement contradicts the information*
NOT GIVEN	*if there is no information on this*

9   Customers can request leaflets on certain topics without paying for postage.

10   Phone calls to ask about service are free.

11   Appointments can be arranged for an exact time.

12   Anglian Water has deadlines for replying to some categories of letter.

13   Customers will receive payment if Anglian Water doesn't fulfil its service commitments.

14   Anglian Water provides help for customers with physical disabilities.

Turn over ▶

SECTION 2   *Questions 15 – 27*

Read the text below and answer Questions 15-20.

What is WorkWise?

WorkWise is a three-year programme which we are about to introduce throughout the company, to give staff different working choices, while at the same time allowing us to reduce expenditure.

WorkWise will become our usual way of working, helping us to make better use of our time, space and technology.

Time
WorkWise provides a range of alternatives. Opportunities for home working, for example, help employees to improve their work/life balance and reduce their travel time and costs.

Space
By making sure all our desks are fully used, through flexi-desking (shared desks), and designing workspaces to support different workstyles, we can rationalise the office accommodation we require and reduce its cost by 20%.

Technology
We will develop our existing technology and implement solutions to enable staff to work flexibly at any of our offices around the country.

WorkWise – what it means for you
You and your team will have a space where you generally work, where visitors can find you, where your post comes to and is collected from and where your possessions are located.

Your team's workspace will reflect realistic desk occupancy levels and how flexibly your team can work. WorkWise is looking to achieve an average team space of seven desks for every ten employees. Understandably some teams will require more, but we know others can work effectively with fewer.

Once your team has been 'WorkWised', you might not have a specific desk allocated to you, and so you will work flexibly by using any available desk. This could be in your team workspace or in another team space. It really will be that flexible. People who no longer have a specific desk will be provided with a portable container to keep their belongings in.

Training
There will be a number of WorkWise training sessions in May:

Venues	Dates
Carter House	9 May 9.30am – 12.30pm
MacDougall House	10 May 1.30pm – 4.30pm

If you would like to attend one of these courses, prior booking is essential. Please use the eForm which can be accessed below, complete it and email it to the helpdesk. You will require approval from your manager, and a budget code, which can be obtained by going to the Finance Office.

Once the helpdesk has all the relevant information, you will receive confirmation by email. Please print that out and take it with you to the training session.

Questions 15 – 20

Complete the notes below.

*Choose **NO MORE THAN TWO WORDS** from the text for each answer.*

Write your answers in boxes 15-20 on your answer sheet.

WorkWise scheme

Introduction

- staff can save time and money by choosing the option of **15** ....
- WorkWise will reduce the company's expenditure on office accommodation
- the company will build on its **16** .... to allow staff to work in a variety of locations

Team workspace

- where staff can meet any visitors
- staff without own desk will be given a storage container for their possessions, which is **17** ....

Booking training

- complete booking form
- get authorisation and a **18** ....
- send form to the **19** ....
- take the email giving **20** .... to training session

Turn over ▶

Read the text below and answer Questions 21-27.

Ottawa City Council

Employee Code of Conduct

Conflict of interest: definition

A conflict of interest occurs when, while carrying out his/her duties, an employee of the City is required to deal with a matter in which he/she has a direct or indirect interest.

A *direct* interest can occur when an employee may gain, or appear to gain, some financial or personal benefit, or avoid financial or personal loss.

An *indirect* interest may arise when the potential benefit or loss would be experienced by another person or organisation having a relationship with the employee. This could be a friend or family member, or a business in which the employee has acquired shares.

These benefits, losses, interests and relationships are generally – but not necessarily – financial in nature. A conflict of interest arises when an employee's activities could benefit a personal interest to the disadvantage of the City's interests. Any behaviour which is, or could be seen as, a conflict of interest is prohibited, and the employee will face disciplinary proceedings.

Examples of conflicts of interest

Examples of potential conflicts of interest include the following:

- **Buying property or goods from the City**

An employee may only submit an offer to purchase City property or goods when these are being sold at public auction. However, employees are not permitted to take part in the public auction of vehicles sold by the City.

- **Choice of suppliers**

The choice of suppliers of goods and services to the City must be based on competitive considerations of quality, price, service and benefit to the City. Contracts will be awarded in a fair and legal manner. The City's policies and established procedure for selecting suppliers must be followed. It is forbidden for an employee to use his/her knowledge to influence this process for direct or indirect personal gain.

Breach of the Code of Conduct

Any employee who believes he/she or another employee is not acting in accordance with this Code of Conduct must report the matter. The procedure for disclosing a breach (or potential breach) is described in the relevant section of the Code.

Post-employment conflict of interest

After ceasing to be employed by the City, employees are not permitted to act in such a way as to benefit improperly from their previous employment.

Questions 21 – 27

Complete the sentences below.

Choose **ONE WORD ONLY** from the text for each answer.

Write your answers in boxes 21-27 on your answer sheet.

21 An indirect interest may occur when an employee's actions affect a company in which he/she owns ………… .

22 Personal benefits arising from a conflict of interest are usually, though not always, ………… ones.

23 ………… action may be taken against an employee acting in a way that creates a conflict of interest.

24 Employees are not allowed to buy ………… of any kind from the City, even at public auction.

25 When choosing suppliers, employees must follow the ………… and standard procedure of the City.

26 Employees must report any ………… of the Code.

27 Employees must not take improper advantage of their past ………… with the City when they have left.

Turn over ▶

SECTION 3   Questions 28 – 40

Read the text on pages 10 and 11 and answer Questions 28-40.

Meet the Organoleptics
People who sip, taste and sniff for a living

A   Paul Fisher sits at a circular table. Before him are two dozen cups of Java coffee of various hues and tastes. The president of Tristao Trading, coffee importers in New York, is preparing to 'cup'.

He raises a spoon to his lips and tastes. He will rank each sample for body, flavour, grade, colour, degree of moisture and acidity. He gives high marks for the soft fruitiness of one, rejects the oily smell and taste of another. After each sampling, he avails himself of the spit sink attached to the table. He decides whether the Kenyan AA batch ordered by one of America's top coffee companies gets a high enough grade to make it to the market.

Fisher is an organoleptic, a person who uses his senses of smell and taste to make a living. Organoleptics sip soft drinks, taste teas, taste wines and test perfume performance.

B   Where do companies find these skilled workers? You might imagine huge recruitment campaigns on university campuses, seeking students with large nostrils and sensitive palates. Not even close. Most firms hire tasters and smellers based simply on the fact that these people like the work; anyone with a normal sense of taste and smell can learn to do the job.

According to John Monsell at the Chemical Senses Center in Philadelphia, virtually all humans are born with an ability to detect sweet, sour, bitter and salty compounds. However, Monsell finds there is a genetic component to having an excellent sense of taste.

C   Most of what we call taste involves smelling from the back of the throat and up into the top of the nose. Smell contributes so much to our appreciation of food that most of us could not recognise our favourite dishes relying on taste alone. For example, if you hold your nose and eat an apple and an onion, they taste the same (although an onion might make your tongue sting).

The average person can detect at least 10,000 odours. Being able to identify those smells is another story. If blindfolded, most people can put a name ('roses', 'fish', 'oak') to fewer than a hundred scents.

D   Organoleptics come from all sorts of backgrounds. Peter Goggi, president of Royal Estates, the tea-buying arm of Lipton, began his career as a research chemist.

'I used to bring samples down to the tea-tasters and listen to their comments,' he recalls. 'I started tasting with them, and thought it might be a good job.' To get some training, he moved to England, then to Kenya. 'The best way to learn,' says Goggi, 'is to taste and taste and taste. I would do about a thousand teas a day.'

'We sip the tea and spit it out,' Goggi explains. One good turn around the mouth will tell an expert taster all he or she needs to know. 'The important thing is to evaluate tea in the same way from cup to cup,' he says. 'We brew the tea for six minutes and taste it with a teaspoon of skimmed milk to bring out the colour.'

E Jack Wild's job isn't quite so refreshing. He had a degree in biochemistry when he went to work at Hill Top Research in 1958. The consumer-products market was taking off then, thanks to postwar technology and increased disposable income. People were beginning to worry about odours.

Hill Top Research tests products for eliminating bad odours. People who volunteer to take part in a test are paid not to use soaps or perfumes for ten days. After each participant has been sprayed with deodorant, the researchers start the ranking process. According to Wild, descriptive ability is not important, since being able to say an odour reminds you of one thing or another is not necessary.

F James Bell started as a clerk at Givaudan Roure, leaders in the creation and manufacture of perfume. Put through a smelling test, Bell did well and was sent to a special school in France. 'I had to learn to identify about 2800 synthetic and 140 natural materials,' Bell says.

Today, Bell is vice-president and senior perfumer of Givaudan Roure. He recognises as many as 5000 scents and must be able to devise special orders requested by leading perfume companies. They want something 'beautiful' or 'fresh', and Bell takes it from there.

When the experts at Givaudan Roure were asked to develop a men's fragrance named after Michael Jordan, the famous basketballer, Bell's perfumery team went to work and identified four core themes – Cool (in honour of Jordan's boyhood home in North Carolina), Fairway (for his love of golf), Home Run (a leather note to represent Jordan's interest in baseball) and Rare Air (celebrating his basketball achievements). The resulting fragrance has become a top-selling men's brand.

G Bell is one of the few in his field who believe natural ability is a pre-requisite for maximising one's sensibilities. 'You start with a superior sense of smell, but then you must train it, like a concert pianist.'

'Perfume,' he continues, 'is like writing music. It has a base note, a midnote and a top note. You smell the top note initially, the midnotes enhance the top note, and the base note brings it all together.'

We owe a real debt to all those organoleptics out there. They make our world smell a little better and taste a little fresher. And just what do they ask of you? Not much. Just that once in a while, we take the time to stop and smell the rose-scented room freshener.

Turn over ▶

Questions 28 – 32

The text has seven sections, **A-G**.

Which section contains the following information?

*Write the correct letter, **A-G**, in boxes 28-32 on your answer sheet.*

NB   *You may use any letter more than once.*

28   the two parts of the body which we use to taste food

29   different kinds of drink that organoleptics taste

30   the basic tastes which everyone can recognise

31   the qualities of a certain beverage

32   the components combined to make a new product

Questions 33 – 37

Do the following statements agree with the information given in the text?

In boxes 33-37 on your answer sheet, write

TRUE   *if the statement agrees with the information*
FALSE   *if the statement contradicts the information*
NOT GIVEN   *if there is no information on this*

33   Oiliness is considered a good flavour in coffee.

34   The average person can name thousands of smells.

35   Participants in smell tests at Hill Top Research are required to avoid using certain products.

36   Most perfumes are made from natural materials.

37   Perfume designers must be able to write clear descriptions of fragrances.

Questions 38 – 40

Look at the following views expressed in the text (Questions 38-40) and the list of people below.

*Match each view with the correct person, **A-E**.*

*Write the correct letter, **A-E**, in boxes 38-40 on your answer sheet.*

38   Both natural ability and training are important.

39   Being able to describe a difference is not important.

40   It is important to keep your method exactly the same.

List of People

A   James Bell
B   Peter Goggi
C   John Monsell
D   Jack Wild
E   Paul Fisher

Candidate Name _____

Candidate Number

INTERNATIONAL ENGLISH LANGUAGE TESTING SYSTEM   0380/2

General Training Writing

PRACTICE MATERIALS   Example 1   1 hour

Additional materials:
    Writing answer booklet

Time   1 hour

INSTRUCTIONS TO CANDIDATES

Do not open this question paper until you are told to do so.

Write your name and candidate number in the spaces at the top of this page.

Read the instructions for each task carefully.

Answer both of the tasks.

Write at least 150 words for Task 1.

Write at least 250 words for Task 2.

Write your answers in the answer booklet.

Write clearly in pen or pencil. You may make alterations, but make sure your work is easy to read.

At the end of the test, hand in both this question paper and your answer booklet.

INFORMATION FOR CANDIDATES

There are **two** tasks on this question paper.

Task 2 contributes twice as much as Task 1 to the Writing score.

PV1

© UCLES 2010

WRITING TASK 1

You should spend about 20 minutes on this task.

You have heard about plans to build new apartments in a public park near your home. You want to give your opinion about this.

Write a letter to the editor of your local newspaper. In your letter

- *explain how you learnt about these plans*
- *say what you think of the park*
- *give your opinion on the plans*

Write at least 150 words.

You do **NOT** need to write any addresses.

Begin your letter as follows:

Dear Sir or Madam,

WRITING TASK 2

You should spend about 40 minutes on this task.

Write about the following topic:

> *Even though doctors all over the world agree that fast food is bad for people's health, more and more people are eating it.*
>
> *Why are more people eating fast food?*
>
> *What can be done about this problem?*

Give reasons for your answer and include any relevant examples from your own knowledge or experience.

Write at least 250 words.

INTERNATIONAL ENGLISH LANGUAGE TESTING SYSTEM **0380/2**

General Training Writing

PRACTICE MATERIALS   **Example 2**   1 hour

Additional materials:
  Writing answer booklet

Time   1 hour

INSTRUCTIONS TO CANDIDATES

Do not open this question paper until you are told to do so.

Write your name and candidate number in the spaces at the top of this page.

Read the instructions for each task carefully.

Answer both of the tasks.

Write at least 150 words for Task 1.

Write at least 250 words for Task 2.

Write your answers in the answer booklet.

Write clearly in pen or pencil. You may make alterations, but make sure your work is easy to read.

At the end of the test, hand in both this question paper and your answer booklet.

INFORMATION FOR CANDIDATES

There are **two** tasks on this question paper.

Task 2 contributes twice as much as Task 1 to the Writing score.

PV1

© UCLES 2010

WRITING TASK 1

You should spend about 20 minutes on this task.

You work in an international company. You need to take some time off work.

Write a letter to your employer. In your letter

- *explain why you need this time off*
- *give details of when you want the time off*
- *say who can do your work when you are away*

Write at least 150 words.

You do **NOT** need to write any addresses.

Begin your letter as follows:

Dear .... ,

WRITING TASK 2

You should spend about 40 minutes on this task.

Write about the following topic:

Some people think that wild animals should not be kept in zoos. Others believe that there are good reasons for having zoos.

Discuss both these views and give your own opinion.

Give reasons for your answer and include any relevant examples from your own knowledge or experience.

Write at least 250 words.

Speaking Test

Time: 11–14 minutes

Format: oral interview between examiner and candidate

Content: 3 parts

Part 1 Introduction and interview
(4–5 minutes)

The examiner introduces him/herself and asks you to introduce yourself and confirm your identity.

The examiner asks you general questions on some familiar topics, e.g. home, family, work, studies, interests.

Part 2 Individual long turn
(3–4 minutes, including 1 minute preparation time)

The examiner gives you a card which asks you to talk about a particular topic and which includes points that you can cover in your talk.

You are given one minute to prepare to talk about the topic on the card. You can make some notes to help you if you wish.

You talk for one to two minutes on the topic.

The examiner then asks you one or two questions on the same topic to finish this part of the test.

Part 3 Two-way discussion
(4–5 minutes)

The examiner asks you further questions which are connected to the topic of Part 2.

These questions give you an opportunity to discuss more abstract issues and ideas.

All Speaking tests are recorded.

The practice materials on page 56 give you an example of the kinds of questions and tasks you could be asked to respond to in the Speaking test.

Speaking Test Practice Materials

Part 1

Example

Let's talk about weekends.

- What do you usually do at the weekend?
- What do you think you'll do next weekend?
- Do you enjoy your weekends now more than you did when you were a child?
- How important is it for you to relax at the end of the week?

Part 2

Candidate task card:

Describe a special gift or present you gave to someone.

You should say:

who you gave the gift to
what the gift was
where you got it from

and explain why this gift was special.

You will have to talk about the topic for 1 to 2 minutes.
You have 1 minute to think about what you are going to say.
You can make some notes to help you if you wish.

Rounding-off questions:

- Did you tell other people about this gift?
- Do you enjoy giving gifts?

Part 3

Example

Let's consider first of all giving gifts in families.

- On what occasions do family members give gifts to each other?
- Is giving gifts important in families?

Let's consider giving gifts in society.

- What situations in business are there when people might give gifts?
- How important is gift giving for a country's economy?

Let's move on to international gifts or international aid.

- What sort of aid do governments give to other countries?
- What do you think motivates governments to give aid to other countries?

How to Mark the Listening and Reading Practice Tests

Each question in the Listening and Reading tests is worth one mark.

Questions which require letter/Roman numeral answers

- For questions where the answers are letters or Roman numerals, you should write *only* the number of answers required. For example, if the answer is a single letter or numeral you should write only one answer. If you write more letters or numerals than are required, your answer is *incorrect*.

Questions which require answers in the form of words or numbers

- You may write your answers in upper or lower case.

- Words in brackets are *optional* – they are correct, but not necessary. If you write any other extra words that are not on the answer key, your answer is *incorrect*.

- Alternative answers are separated by a slash (/). If you write any of the alternative answers, your answer is *correct*.

- If you are asked to write an answer using a certain number of words and/or (a) number(s), you will be penalised if you exceed this. For example, if a question specifies an answer using NO MORE THAN THREE WORDS and the correct answer is 'black leather coat', the answer 'coat of black leather' is *incorrect*.

- In questions where you are expected to complete a gap, you should only copy the necessary missing word(s) or number(s) onto the answer sheet. For example, to complete 'in the ... ', where the correct answer is 'morning', the answer 'in the morning' is *incorrect*.

- All answers require correct spelling, including any words in brackets. You should take care, therefore, when copying your answers onto the answer sheets.

- Both US and UK spelling are acceptable and are included in the answer key.

- All standard alternatives for numbers, dates and currencies are acceptable.

- All standard abbreviations are acceptable.

Listening and Reading Practice Test Answer Keys

Listening

Section 1

1	(the) 26th
2	7.00
3	circle
4	A21 -/to (A)24
5	Mastercard
6	3290 5876 4401 2899
7	Whitton
8	42 South
9	SW2 5GE
10	headphones/earphones

Section 2

11	D
12	F
13	I
14	B
15	E
16	A
17	G
18	arm band
19	an ambulance/ambulances
20	yellow ticket(s)

Section 3

21–23 **IN ANY ORDER**

	B
	D
	F
24	A
25	B
26	C
27	A
28	March
29	secretary
30	computer office

Section 4

31	coast(s)/shore
32	garbage/rubbish/waste
33	summer
34	fish
35	checked
36	boat
37	camera
38	released/freed
39	B
40	A

Academic Reading

Section 1

1	ii
2	viii
3	v
4	i
5	iii
6	ix
7	New Zealand/NZ carrageen(s)
8	agar
9	seameal
10	cough mixtures
11	B
12	C
13	A

Section 2

14	crochet hook
15	(paired) leaflets/leaves
16	thorn
17	(tapered) steps
18	TRUE
19	TRUE
20	FALSE
21	TRUE
22	NOT GIVEN
23	FALSE

24–26 **IN ANY ORDER**

	C
	D
	F

Section 3

27	A
28	D
29	C
30	B
31	C
32	B
33	D
34	B
35	A
36	C
37	H
38	L
39	A
40	I

General Training Reading

Section 1

1	C
2	D
3	F
4	E
5	B
6	A
7	D
8	B
9	TRUE
10	FALSE
11	FALSE
12	TRUE
13	TRUE
14	TRUE

Section 2

15	home working
16	(existing) technology
17	portable
18	budget code
19	helpdesk
20	confirmation
21	shares
22	financial
23	Disciplinary
24	vehicles
25	policies
26	breach
27	employment

Section 3

28	C
29	A
30	B
31	A
32	F
33	FALSE
34	FALSE
35	TRUE
36	NOT GIVEN
37	NOT GIVEN
38	A
39	D
40	B

Listening Tapescript

SECTION 1

You will hear a conversation between a customer and a booking officer at a theatre.

F: Hello, Theatre Royal Plymouth.

M: Oh hello – I'd like to make a booking, please.

F: Yes. What is it you want to see?

M: *The Impostor.*

F: Right. And which day did you want to come?

M: Friday the 25th.

F: Just a moment and I'll check availability on the computer. Oh, sorry, we're fully booked for that performance.

M: Oh dear. What about the following day then?

F: The 26th? Yes, that's OK. We've got two performances on that day, one at 3.30 and one at 7. Which would you prefer?

M: Oh, the later one, please.

F: How many people?

M: Well, there are four of us.

F: Are there any concessions, any children?

M: I'm not sure. My daughters are 15 and 12. Do they get concessions?

F: Only the 12-year-old I'm afraid. So that's one child and three adults. Any idea where you'd like to sit? Stalls or circle?

M: Er ...

F: Tickets for the stalls are a bit more expensive – £12 for adults and £8.50 for children. The circle costs £10.50 and £6.50.

M: Do you get a good view from the circle?

F: Oh, yes. And in fact we've got some seats left at the front, if you'd like those.

M: Right, we'll go for those then.

F: Right. That's seats A 21 to 24 then. They're very good seats.

M: That sounds fine.

F: So let's see. That comes to £38 altogether for the tickets. How do you want to collect them? Shall I put them in the post? They'd be sent today by first class mail, and there'd be an additional charge of £1 to cover postage and administration. Or do you want to get them from the box office yourself?

M: Oh yes. Could you send them please?

F: No problem. That'll be £39 altogether. Could I just take your card details? What kind of card is it? Visa? Switch?

M: Mastercard.

F: OK. And the number?

M: It's 3290 5876 4401 2899.

F: 28 double 9. OK. And the name on the card please?

M: It's Mr J Whitton – W-H-I-doubleT-O-N.

F: N for 'never' or M for 'mother'?

M: N for 'never'.

F: Thank you. And now, I've nearly finished, but I just need your address and post code.

M: Yes. It's 42 South Street.

F: OK. Is that Plymouth?

M: London.

F: And the post code?

M: It's SW2 5GE.

F: That's fine then. The tickets should be with you tomorrow. Is there anything else I can do for you?

M: Yes. I was wondering if I could get regular information about what's on.

F: Certainly. I can just add your name to our mailing list. Would that be OK?

M: That would be very good. Yes please. Oh, and there is something else, sorry. One of our group is hard of hearing and I've heard that you can supply special headphones.

F: That's right. As long as you tell us in advance, we can always do that. I'll book those for you now, and you can just collect them from the box office before the show.

M: Thanks very much for your help.

F: No problem. Thank you for calling.

M: Thank you. Bye.

SECTION 2

You will hear the organiser of a rock festival talking to the exhibitors and performers at a planning meeting.

Good evening, everyone!

I'm glad you could all make this planning meeting for what promises to be the biggest and most colourful free rock festival ever held in the south-east! So whether you're a performer, a craft exhibitor or an artist, we all extend a big welcome to you.

Could we turn first to the plan so I can familiarise you with the layout of the site – which as you know is an old football stadium – we're really lucky to have so much space this year. You can see the main gate at the bottom of the plan – have you found it? – that's where most visitors will enter. It's also the entrance for those taking part in the craft fair: we've set the stalls just inside the gate on the left, in a circle.

If you walk straight ahead from the gate along the path without turning right, you'll come to some steps up to the football stadium. On the left of the steps is the Fringe Stage. This is for alternative artistes – they include folk singers, poets and other acts which are more suited to a smaller stage – and they should also enter by the main gate. On the opposite side of the steps is a restaurant, and adjoining that is the main festival information point. Here you can get extra programmes and up-to-the-minute information about events, and you can discuss any last-minute problems – although we hope everything will be running smoothly when the festival opens.

Right, coming back to the plan, you go up the stairs to the stadium. The entrance for the rock bands is on the far side, and on your right is the main stage, which will have powerful illumination and amplification throughout the weekend. There will probably be TV vehicles adjacent – that's in this area only – for recording purposes.

If you look at the outside of the plan, you can see a third gate for exhibitors opening onto a side path. A little way down the path, before you get to the trees, is the building where the Art Exhibition's being housed. Then finally there's just one more building marked on your plan – quite near the main gate. It's divided into lock-up garages. So I hope you now feel quite familiar with the main festival area.

We also hope that you'll have received your welcome pack. In it, you should find two parking tickets for yourself and anyone assisting you, an arm band to indicate that you are an official visitor, one of our brilliant yellow badges with the new festival logo, a festival programme, and several sheets of information that we'd ask you to study carefully before the event.

Please could you note that all setting up of stalls, displays and so on should be completed by 9.30 a.m. and that unfortunately we won't be able to allow any vehicles to enter the festival area after that time. Yes, it's a big site – but even a few vehicles parked in the wrong place can block the paths. With crowds of people – and we are expecting several thousand – this can merely be a nuisance; but if there's an emergency and access for an ambulance is blocked, the situation will become not just annoying but also dangerous. And don't forget it could be your mother or your child who needs help.

Several exhibitors and craftspeople have asked us if any provision can be made for overnight storage of tables, chairs and display items rather than having to take them home and bring them again. We're pleased to say that a limited amount of space has been made available in the building near the main gate. You'll be issued with a yellow ticket to reclaim your property – similar to the red parking tickets, so do check you bring the right one! – but please understand that this is entirely at your own risk as we can take no responsibility for items lost or damaged.

I think that's all I have to say at this point but thank you all for your attention!

SECTION 3

You will hear a discussion between a business student called Marco and his personal tutor about the courses that Marco should take.

T: Hi Marco, come in.

M: Thanks. I've got a bit stuck trying to select courses for next semester. Could you help me, please?

T: Of course. Sit down. First of all, most people just go for the areas of business that they're interested in, but – even if something doesn't look very stimulating – it's important that you can use it once you get a job. It's not much good choosing areas that aren't going to be helpful later on.

M: Right. I want to go into management, so I'll need to think about that. And should I start specialising in a particular area yet?

T: I don't think that's wise, at this stage. It's better to aim for a wide variety of subjects, especially as management covers so many possibilities. You shouldn't be limiting your choices for later on.

M: Yes I see.

T: You should also look at how the course is made up – will you have regular seminars and tutorials, for example, as well as lectures?

M: OK. Some of the lecturers are quite big names in their fields, aren't they? Should I aim to go to their courses?

T: Well remember that the lecturers who aren't well-known may still be very good teachers! I'd say we have a consistently high standard of teaching in this department, so you don't need to worry about it.

M: Good. Well that's a great help.

T: Now last time we met, you mentioned doing Team Management, didn't you?

M: That's right. I'm still quite keen on the idea.

T: The trouble is that because of changes in the content of various courses, Team Management overlaps with the Introduction to Management course you took in your first year. So what you'd learn from it would be too little for the amount of time you'd have to spend on it.

M: I'll drop that idea, then. Have you had a chance to look at the outline I wrote for my finance dissertation? I left it in your pigeonhole last week.

T: Yes. Why exactly do you want to write a dissertation, instead of taking the finance modules? It'll be pretty demanding.

M: Well, I'm quite prepared to do the extra work, because I'm keen to investigate something in depth, instead of just skating across the surface. I realise that a broader knowledge base may be more useful to my career, but I'm really keen to do this.

T: Right. Well I had a quick look through your outline, and the first thing that struck me was that you'll have to be careful how you set about it, as the way you've organised it seems unnecessarily complex. The data that you want to collect and analyse is potentially valuable, but you'll need to narrow down the subject matter to make the whole thing manageable.

M: OK, I'll have another look at it. I was talking to Professor Briggs about it yesterday, and I got some more ideas then. For part of the dissertation I was thinking of trying to persuade finance managers from three or four companies to let me ask them about their company finances. If not I think I'll have to change to another topic.

T: Well go ahead then. I could give you some names.

M: Thanks.

T: Now let's talk about practicalities. Your dissertation must be finalised by the end of May, so you should aim to finish the first draft by the end of March. Is that feasible?

M: Yes, it shouldn't be a problem. I'll need to register for the dissertation, won't I? Is that with the Registrar's department?

T: No, it's internal to this department, so you just need to let the secretary know. Do that as soon as you're sure you're going to write the dissertation.

M: OK.

T: Then to analyse your statistics, you're going to need some suitable software. If I were you, I'd drop in to the computer office and ask them for a copy.

M: Right. So if I revise my outline, can I ...

SECTION 4

You will hear a talk about a research project on the tiger shark.

Good morning, everyone. Today, I'm going to talk about the research project I've been involved in on the tiger shark.

First of all, some background information. The tiger shark, also known as the leopard shark, is often thought to have got its name from its aggressive nature, but in actual fact, it's called that because it has dark bands similar to those on a tiger's body.

It is a huge creature growing up to lengths of six and a half metres. It can be found just about everywhere throughout the world's temperate and tropical seas, but it is most often found along the coast, rather than the open sea.

In terms of feeding, tiger sharks tend to be most active at night and are solitary hunters. Their preferred prey includes other sharks, turtles, seabirds and dolphins, to name but a few. However, it's not uncommon to find garbage in its stomach. This is because it tends to feed in areas such as harbours and river inlets, where there is a lot of human activity.

Now to the project itself. We are particularly interested in some studies that had been done in the Raine Island area. Observations here have shown that there is a large population of tiger sharks present in the summer, during the turtle nesting season. However, during the winter months the sharks disappear – so we decided to do some of our own research there.

The first step was to tag a number of sharks so that we could follow their movements. To do this, we first needed to catch the sharks. Early in the morning, we baited lines with large bits of fish and set them in place. These lines were then checked every three or four hours. If no sharks were caught, the baits were replaced. Once a shark had been caught on one of the baited hooks, it was pulled in close to the boat and secured so that we could carry out a number of brief activities to aid our research. This usually took no more than about ten minutes and was carried out as carefully as possible to minimise any stress to the shark. Each of the tiger sharks that we caught was measured and fitted with an identification tag and also a small amount of tissue was taken for genetic studies. For some larger sharks over three metres long, we also inserted into the belly a special acoustic tag capable of sending satellite signals, while on other large sharks we attached a camera to the dorsal fin, to enable us to study the behaviour and habitat use of the sharks. After this, the shark was released, and we were able to follow its movements.

So what was the purpose of all this tagging? Well, while we were already familiar with some aspects of the tiger sharks' behaviour and food sources, what we hoped to do in this project was to see exactly what factors affected the migration patterns of tiger sharks and whether it was in fact food, weather and reproductive needs.

These are some of our findings: On February 21st a large female shark, whom we named Natalie, was attracted to our research boat at the northern tip of Raine Island and fitted with one of the satellite tags I've just mentioned. No transmissions were received from Natalie between April 2nd and April 29th indicating that she didn't surface to feed during this period. The area in which she was last reported is very shallow, suggesting that she may have changed her feeding preferences during this period to focus on prey found on the sea floor.

We also made a number of other discoveries thanks to the various transmitters we used. It seems that tiger sharks move back and forth between the ocean floor and the surface quite often. This may help the sharks conserve energy while they swim, but it probably also helps them hunt, since this movement back and forth maximises its chances of not being detected by its prey until the last minute.

So far our findings have not been conclusive. However, we have gained some very interesting insights into the behaviour of tiger sharks and are now hoping to develop our research further.

Interpreting your Scores

Your score in Listening

Scores 28 and above

If you have strictly followed the guidelines on page 3, you are likely to get an acceptable score on the IELTS Listening test under examination conditions, but remember that different institutions will find different scores acceptable.

Scores 13–27

You may not get an acceptable score on the IELTS Listening test under examination conditions and we recommend that you think about having more lessons or practice before you take IELTS.

Scores 0–12

You are highly unlikely to get an acceptable score on the IELTS Listening test under examination conditions and we recommend that you spend a lot of time improving your English before you take IELTS.

Your score in Academic Reading

Scores 29 and above

If you have strictly followed the guidelines on page 3, you are likely to get an acceptable score on the IELTS Academic Reading test under examination conditions, but remember that different institutions will find different scores acceptable.

Scores 13–28

You may not get an acceptable score on the IELTS Academic Reading test under examination conditions and we recommend that you think about having more lessons or practice before you take IELTS.

Scores 0–12

You are highly unlikely to get an acceptable score on the IELTS Academic Reading test under examination conditions and we recommend that you spend a lot of time improving your English before you take IELTS.

Your score in General Training Reading

Scores 31 and above

If you have strictly followed the guidelines on page 3, you are likely to get an acceptable score on the IELTS General Training Reading test under examination conditions, but remember that different institutions will find different scores acceptable.

Scores 18–30

You may not get an acceptable score on the IELTS General Training Reading test under examination conditions and we recommend that you think about having more lessons or practice before you take IELTS.

Scores 0–17

You are highly unlikely to get an acceptable score on the IELTS General Training Reading test under examination conditions and we recommend that you spend a lot of time improving your English before you take IELTS.

Please note the following:

- The above recommendations are based on the average scores which the majority of institutions and organisations accept. However, different institutions and organisations accept different scores for different purposes. The institution to which you are applying may require a higher or lower score than most other institutions. Please check score requirements for individual institutions on the IELTS website **www.ielts.org**

- Your performance in the real IELTS test will be reported in two ways: there will be a Band Score from 1 to 9 for each of the skills; and an Overall Band Score from 1 to 9. Both the Band Scores for each skill and the Overall Band Score may be reported in whole or half bands. The Overall Band Score is the average of your scores in the four skills. For example, if you score Band 6 for Listening, Band 6 for Reading, Band 5 for Writing and Band 7 for Speaking, your Overall Band Score will be:

$$\frac{6 + 6 + 5 + 7}{4} = \frac{24}{4} = 6$$

You will see from this example that a lower score in one skill can be compensated for by higher scores in the others.

- Institutions or organisations considering your application are advised to look at both the Overall Band Score and the Band Scores for each skill to make sure you have the language skills needed for a particular purpose. For example, if your course has a lot of reading and writing, but no lectures, listening comprehension might not be very important and a score of, say, 5 in Listening might be acceptable if the Overall Band Score was 7. However, for a course where there are lots of lectures and spoken instructions, a score of 5 in Listening might be unacceptable even though the Overall Band Score was 7.

- This Practice Test has been checked so that it is approximately the same level of difficulty as the real IELTS test. However, we cannot guarantee that your score in the Practice Test will be reflected in the real IELTS test. The Practice Test can only give you an idea of your possible future performance and it is up to you to decide whether you are ready to take IELTS.

How Writing is Assessed

The Academic and General Training Writing tests both consist of two tasks, Task 1 and Task 2. Each task is assessed independently.

Writing performance is assessed by certificated examiners who are appointed by the test centre and approved by the British Council or IDP: IELTS Australia.

The examiner rates the candidate's responses using detailed performance descriptors which describe writing performance at the nine IELTS bands. These descriptors apply to both the Academic and General Training Writing tests.

Task 1 responses are assessed on the following four criteria:

Task Achievement
This criterion refers to how appropriately, accurately and relevantly the response fulfils the requirements of the task. Responses must be at least 150 words in length.

Academic Writing Task 1 is an information-transfer task with a defined response which requires candidates to draw on the factual content of a diagram. Candidates are not expected to speculate or explain any areas that lie outside the input material.

General Training Writing Task 1 is also a task with a defined response which requires candidates to write a letter in response to an everyday situation or problem. The input material describes the context and purpose of the letter and the functions candidates should cover in their responses.

Coherence and Cohesion
This criterion refers to the overall clarity and fluency of the message: how the response organises and links information, ideas and language. Coherence refers to the linking of ideas through logical sequencing. Cohesion refers to the varied and appropriate use of cohesive devices (for example, logical connectors, pronouns and conjunctions) to assist in making the references and relationships between and within sentences clear.

Lexical Resource
This criterion refers to the range of vocabulary the candidate uses and the accuracy and appropriacy of that use.

Grammatical Range and Accuracy
This criterion refers to the range and accurate use of the candidate's grammatical resource at sentence level.

Task 2 responses are assessed on the following four criteria:

Task Response
This criterion refers to the candidate's ability to formulate and develop a position in relation to a question or statement. Ideas should be supported by evidence, and examples may be drawn from the candidate's own experience. Responses must be at least 250 words in length.

Coherence and Cohesion
As for Task 1.

Lexical Resource
As for Task 1.

Grammatical Range and Accuracy
As for Task 1.

All criteria have equal weighting.

Task 2 contributes twice as much as Task 1 to the Writing score.

Candidates should note that they will lose marks in Writing if their responses are a) under the minimum word length, b) partly or wholly plagiarised, c) not written as full, connected text (e.g. if the response is in note form, if bullet points are used etc.).

The public version of the Writing band descriptors is available on the IELTS website **www.ielts.org**

Sample Candidate Writing Responses and Examiner Comments

On the following pages, you will find candidate responses to the five Writing Practice Tests. There is one response for each Writing task. Below each response, you will find examiner comments and the Band Scores given.

The examiner guidelines for assessing candidate performance on the Writing test are very detailed. There are many different ways a candidate may achieve a particular Band Score. The candidate responses that follow should not be regarded as definitive examples of any particular Band Score.

Academic Writing Example 1 – Task 1
Sample Response 1

> The charts shows the oil resources held, together with the proportions consumed within the same area each year, in different areas of the world
> It is obvious that the region holding the most oil sources is the Middle East, with 56.52%, over a half of total world oil resources. While in the United States and Asia, the level of oil consumed each year is far more away from the oil resources they hold. The percentage of total world oil consumption of United States and Asia are 23.48% and 26.21% respectively. They are the two highest oil consumption region in the world.
> Another place that is worth mentioned will be the Western Europe. With about twenty percent of total world oil consumption, the Western Europe merely holds less than 1.5% of the oil resources in the world.
>
> Regions that are not mentioned above have the close percentage between oil holding and consuming. Whereas Canada has the higher level of oil holding than consuming, the respective figures are 14.84% and 2.45%.
> Overall, the charts suggest that Middle East is the only majority of oil resources held, while Asia, United States and Western have the highest level of oil resources imported.

Examiner Comments

Band 5.5

This response describes the main points of the bar graphs and provides a summary of their most significant features. However, the figures are not well selected to support or highlight the key features, there are some minor inaccuracies, and details are missing, with only half of the countries on the graphs being mentioned. There is an overall progression to the response, though the middle section could have been structured more clearly and coherently by use of linkers. There are no errors in spelling, but this accuracy is achieved by staying within a limited range of vocabulary, and by relying on repetition of the phrases supplied on the question paper. Grammatical errors occur but are not frequent or serious enough to affect communication, and there is a range of sentence types which includes some complex structures.

Academic Writing Example 1 – Task 2

Sample Response 2

It's generally supposed that the younger people should respect and take care of older people. Nowadays, many people think that the older people are the problem of modern society. However, How people should give the important older people in this present time for preventing the problem in society.

In many countries are facing of this problem because many people are responsible everything in their lifes. For example, One person has many roles in society such as parents, boss and teacher etc. This reason make someone who forget older people. Some countries, many older people live alone which the government has not pension and facilities for them. In my country this is the problem because older population are increasing every year. They don't have a house for living, don't have money and children and cousins don't take care of them. The government must be help them by providing many houses which this case invest a lot of money to making this project.

On the other hand, In some countries, The government help and support the older people for instance, European people have pension and good facilities such as, free for seeing doctor don't paying when taking the public transportation. I totally agree with this view that my country provide it for them It is the good reason

Examiner Comments

Band 4.5

There are two main problems with this response. Firstly, it is too short and does not meet the length requirement for a Task 2 response (a minimum of 250 words). Secondly, most of this response is irrelevant. From the seventh line, it goes off the topic of respect and instead discusses what provisions governments should make for the elderly. Apart from these two major weaknesses, there are some good points about this response. It shows evidence of organisation in terms of an opening paragraph which introduces the topic, and two concluding sentences at the end. Linking devices are quite well used throughout to connect the different ideas (although the response as a whole lacks coherence in relation to the actual question). The vocabulary is the best feature of this writing: in spite of the largely irrelevant argument, there is a sufficient range of words which specifically relate to the topic, and spelling errors are very few. As for grammar, the writer attempts complex structures, but these are faulty, and mistakes occur with even simple present verbs.

Sample Response 3

The diagrams indicate the alterations being made to the school from 2004 to 2024 to accommodate for the predicted increase in student numbers from 600 to 1,000. In 2004 the school only has one car park with a path leading from the main entrance to the sports field. The path seperates the two school buildings which, together with the sports field, are located north. Trees are present north north-east, east and west of the school. In comparison the school planned for 2024 has two carparks and three school buildings. The path in the 2024 plan links building three to buildings one and two, which are planned to be joined together by building infrastructure. A road is envisioned to connect carpark two with carpark one. In addition the sports field will be reduced in size and relocated south of its previous location below carpark two. The surrounding trees remain in similar positions only requiring a few trees to be repositioned or replanted around new infrastructure.

These changes to the school buildings, road, path, carparks and sportsfield aim to house the extra 400 students planned to be attending the school in 2024. The only decrease in size of any part of the school from 2004 to 2024 is the sports field in order to accomodate school building number three.

Examiner Comments

Band 7.5

This is a very accurate description of the two diagrams, which covers every aspect of the information shown. There is nothing inaccurate or irrelevant in this response with regard to content. It has a clear introductory sentence, and a summing-up at the end. The middle section of the response is logically arranged by year, though this first paragraph is rather long and could usefully have been split into three. Cohesive devices are few, but flexible, and help the reader when they are used. The range of vocabulary used is quite wide and precise, and includes several low-frequency items used appropriately. Errors in word choice and spelling occur rarely. A wide range of grammatical structures and all punctuation are accurately used throughout, but this criterion is not a 9 as the choice of tense could be more precise and consistent.

Academic Writing Example 2 – Task 2

Sample Response 4

I MOST DEFINITELY AGREE WITH THIS STATEMENT, AND I AM CONVINCED THAT IF MORE PEOPLE WOULD SHARE THIS AGREEMENT, MANY OF TODAY'S PROBLEMS COULD BE AVOIDED AND, UNDER THE RISK OF SOUNDING CANDID, "THE WORLD WOULD BE A BETTER PLACE".

IF ONE IS AWARE OF THE GENERAL, WESTERN (WELL, GLOBAL REALLY) CIVILIZATIONAL TENDENCY TOWARDS LIVING WITHIN CLOSED GROUPS, ALMOST FROM "BIRTH TO DEATH", ONE MAY FIND THAT ADDRESSING THE SUBJECT AT THE EARLIEST MOMENT POSSIBLE IS A REASONABLE POSSIBILITY OF STARTING TO FIGHT THAT TENDENCY. CHILDREN ARE NATURALLY KEPT, IN THE FIRST FEW YEARS OF THEIR LIVES, IN A VERY LIMITED, CONTROLLED ENVIRONMENT, AND THEN GRADUALLY START OPENING UP TO THE WORLD AROUND THEM. SO IT'S VERY IMPORTANT THAT, WHEN THEY START DOING SO, THEY ALSO BEGIN TO UNDERSTAND WHAT SURROUNDS THEM – PEOPLE, RACES, SOCIAL BACKGROUNDS, FAMILY STRUCTURES, RELIGIOUS BELIEFS, ETC. – AS PART OF THE REAL WORLD WHERE THEY WILL LIVE AND BE CALLED TO CHANGE, IMPROVE OR CONDITION.

THE ALTERNATIVE TO THIS WILL BE, AS IT IS ALREADY TODAY, THAT CHILDREN WILL LIVE MORE AND MORE ISOLATED FROM REALITY IN ALL ITS VARIED, AND SOMETIMES CRUEL, FEATURES. I BELIEVE THESE CHILDREN, NOT HAVING HAD A CHANCE TO DIRECTLY COMMUNICATE AND INTERACT WITH OTHER KINDS OF CHILDREN, WILL FEAR AND EVEN REJECT SUCH DIFFERENCES. IGNORANCE AND MISUNDERSTANDING IS (HAS BEEN

AND WILL BE) ONE IMPORTANT SOURCE OF CONFLICT, AND SOCIAL CONFLICT IN THE FIRST INSTANCE.

I THINK I CAN SAY I WAS FORTUNATE ENOUGH TO HAVE ATTENDED AN ELEMENTARY SCHOOL WHICH WAS CHARACTERIZED, AMONG OTHER THINGS, FOR JUST SUCH A FEATURE: EVEN THOUGH IT WAS A PRIVATE SCHOOL, WHERE PARENTS WHO COULD AFFORD IT HAD TO PAY A SUBSTANTIAL FEE, IT HAD A POLICY OF TAKING IN CHILDREN WITH ALL KINDS OF DIFFERENCES. I GOT ACCOSTUMED TO HAVING COLEAGUES AND FRIEDS OF LOWER SOCIAL BACKGROUNDS (ECONOMICALLY SPEAKING), WHO WHERE STATE-FINANCED TO ATTEND THE SCHOOL; WITH DIFFERENT LEARNING HABILITIES (DEAF, MENTALLY DISAVANTAGED, ETC.); AND OF DIFFERENT ETHNIC BACKGROUNDS (ASIAN AND FROM PORTUGUESE ~~PORTOGHESE~~ AFRICAN EX-COLONIES).

I AM VERY CERTAIN THAT THIS PART OF MY EDUCATION HELPED ME BETTER UNDERSTANDING AND ACCEPTING THE WORLD AROUND ME; STILL NOWADAYS I HAVE ALL KINDS OF FRIENDS AND LIKE TO KNOW THINGS ABOUT ALL KYNDS OF PEOPLE, AND I KNOW NOT EVERYONE AROUND ME DES THE SAME.

Examiner Comments

Band 7

Although the topic could be more precisely introduced, this response opens with a clear statement of the writer's opinion, and goes on to develop its position clearly and logically, right through to the end. The conclusion would possibly be stronger if it referred back to the actual topic rather than being wholly personal. Paragraphs are used to good effect, and the writing flows well, helped by skilful use of referencing pronouns to link sentences. There is quite a wide range of vocabulary used, with a natural feel for style and collocation, although there are also occasional errors in both word choice and spelling. The grammar consists of a wide range of sentence types used flexibly and accurately; though occasional mistakes occur in verb form and word order, these do not impede communication, and the majority of sentences are error free.

Academic Writing Example 3 – Task 1

Sample Response 5

I am going to talk about summarise. Firstly Republic of Korea people workes in Underground probably 22% in this job. In adition, some of people has a Incineration, I think about 9% they are workes in this job. We can see 66% of the people workes in recycling more than hafe of people they did these job. Secondly sweden the must of people they are workes in the underground, In order to 25% of the people workes in the recycling. Also 20% of Sweden people workes in the Incineration.

Thirdly United kingdom they have more than two jobs. For example, British people likes to worke in the Underground because, the contry has a lots of things to do wit in the Underground. that's more the Dumping at sea in the summer. Also the chemical treatment and Incinevebion they are needed as much as any job.

Examiner Comments

Band 4

This response illustrates the need to read the question very carefully before beginning to write. Due to a misunderstanding of the three pie charts given, this writer does not describe the actual topic, but discusses types of job instead. This means that all the information stated in this response is inaccurate. However, the response is organised and some connectives are used to link the sentences together – this is the strongest feature of the response. Even so, it is not always easy to follow the overall development. There are many spelling mistakes on even basic words, and the range of vocabulary is very limited. Errors in sentence structure and grammar are frequent and there are few attempts at complex sentences. Although some structures within sentences are accurate, no whole sentence is correct, and this causes some strain for the reader.

Sample Response 6

Nowaday, the technolodge is much developed than before, and people owened a car is quite normal, however, ~~when~~ the car gives us more easier life also takes many problems, every year has many people dead in traffic accidents. Some people think that reduce ~~traffic~~ transport accidents the key is strict punishments. I think that is the way and can be done. for driving offenses

For me, traffic accident is ~~not~~ well-known, as my ~~parent~~ father ~~is a~~ had met an accident ~~a it~~, and because ~~of~~ he drove too ~~wins~~ fast and ~~be too~~ too tired. If ~~I~~ I told him strict punishments, don't so hurry, ~~he might be this~~ this accident, might be should n't ~~be~~ happen. When people always think that speed can take us ~~exacteting~~, wonderful feeling and forget their family worried about them, their future should be fantastic if they take care. Strict punishment is ~~en ~~ ~~estrict~~ especially important.

However, On the ~~other~~ hand, many ways can improve road safety, for example, more educate in usual life, more advesting On TV, radio, newspapers, limit speed on the road, stronger fines. I think that the most important is foundation, everything happened, nothing can do more, ~~but~~ before it happen, we can learn a plenty of from ~~others~~ ~~experineces~~ accidents, why we drive so fast, why we forget the friends, family's love and worry. Father have to educate children, ~~when you~~ because of yours mistake, you may be broken two ~~family~~ families or more families's happiness. This responsibility is huge that you can't imagin. So I think foundation is the most ~~need any~~ need thing to do. ~~let~~ Every one need know about that car or other transports we invented ~~is~~ our life to be easier, not ~~bring~~ us sad, many years ago, not so developed society as now, but the world still turned very good, people's life still happy. Why when the technoledge become so develop, lots of unhappy things happened, government should think about it, also our ~~people~~ need attention this problem, than our life will be more comfortable and more ~~safe~~ safety.

Examiner Comments

Band 3.5

This answer is an attempt to address the three parts of the prompt (two opposing views and the writer's own opinion) but there are few relevant ideas. Instead, the writing is somewhat anecdotal and the last paragraph in particular is vague and seems to be dealing with a different topic, namely technology. The writing is laid out in paragraphs, but within each paragraph, ideas are not clearly grouped and seem to be repeated across paragraphs. Despite the use of linking words there is no logical sequencing of ideas, and they are difficult to relate to each other, so the argument is very difficult for the reader to follow. There are some relevant words, but control of spelling is so poor that several words are unintelligible. When we look at the grammar, some structures are correct but overall many sentences are lacking a main verb, so that although the meaning can be followed, this is only managed with difficulty.

Sample Response 7

Dear Sir or Madam,

It is Mohammad khatib, one of the fans of your newspaper. I am writing this letter to you to let you know of some, I hope, rumors I have heard recently about construction plans in our popular public park.

As you know, this is the only park within our immediate vicinity, and many people go there for refreshment. and relaxing So many children also play in this park with their peers. I have recently heard from some of my neighbors that Royal construction company intends to build some apartment blocks in the park. At first I did not take it serious until yesterday that I saw some engineers measuring and calculating different dimensions of the park.

We all like our local park including its beautiful fountain, its playground and amusing facilities for children. So, I, as the representative of most of the neighbors have collected signatures against this project.

Therefore, we, as local neighbors, disagree with the plan and ask you to please kindly write an article about the disadvantages of this action and express our great disapproval of the plan. We are looking forward to seeing your article as our voice soon.

Thanks from your cooperation in advance.

Yours faithfully,
Mohammad Khatib

Examiner Comments

Band 7.5

This letter covers all three parts of the question very well. Its content is relevant and well illustrated, and the writer's purpose is very clear. The tone of the letter is also consistently appropriate throughout: polite and suitable for addressing the editor of a newspaper. It is easy for the reader to follow the message of this letter, because it has a clear structure and the ideas are presented in a logical order. Connecting words, referencing and skilful paragraphing all contribute to the coherence of the letter. Lexical errors occasionally occur in word form, word choice and spelling. However the grammar is highly accurate.

Sample Response 8

Unfortunately as the world goes on improving people more and more are eager to have fast foods. It's now a kind of habit for kids and also adults to spend their leisure time at fast food restaurants. On my opinion one of the major reason of using fast foods in many countries is the shortage of time that people face with. It should be investigated properly to solve this subject.

As a matter of fact nowadays people in all over the world ought to work outdoors more than before. You know that living expenses are so high that spouses should work together in order to gain more. Therefore they have little time to spend on cooking.

Another reason is the great advertisements which being done by TV programs or magazines, tempting every body to use fast food. Now, parents are paying more attention to their children's needs regardless of how much logically they are. They are about to provide their needs even if children are addicted to take fast foods or so.

You know that obesity, high cholestrol, diabete and laziness are some outcomes of fast food, and if it is neglected may lead to serious problems.

I think nutrition experts are expected to offer more warning programs to people about this matter. Government should spend a special budget on giving people some solution about this subjects. For example making animation programs bearing warning messages for the children is one way to make them aware of it's fate. Or cooking programs which learn how to prepare a healthy food in short time seemed to be useful in solving this problem.

In conclusion, it needs to plan a serious plan and spend more time and budget to find a way on solving the peril of its widespread. I hope every person would be more careful about his or her health especially on nutrition case.

Examiner Comments

Band 6

Both parts of the question are addressed in this response, and the content is appropriate for the topic. The writer's position is clear, and there are plenty of relevant ideas which are developed and supported. These are arranged in an organised way, and paragraphing is helpfully used, so that the response as a whole generally progresses coherently to the conclusion. There are errors in word choice and spelling, but the range of vocabulary is quite wide and includes some less common words which specifically relate to the topic. With regard to the grammar, there is a mix of sentence types, but errors occur with plurals, prepositions, word order and punctuation, and with passives and verbs in complex structures.

General Training Writing Example 2 – Task 1

Sample Response 9

Dear Mr. White,

I am writing this letter to explain why I need to take two weeks off and the time about my holidays.

I started work in our company at July 2008. since then I did not go back to China. I found it out in the next few weeks our department do not has lots work to do. So I think maybe it is a good chance for me to take two weeks off and go back to China enjoy the holidays with my family and friends.

I checked the next available ticket will be at 01 August 2009, so I am thinkig take my holiday from 01/08/2009 to 15/08/2009. I talked with Brian Kiby today, he said he will cover my work during the time when I in China, and I will bring my laptop with me, everyday I will check my emails and will resolve any problems Brian can not fix.

Thanks again for your attention, I am looking forward to hearing from you soon.

Yours Sincerely

Examiner Comments

Band 6

This letter addresses the requirements of the task in that it adequately covers all three of the bullet points, and the writer's purpose is generally clear. The tone of the letter is suitable for writing to an employer, and all of the content is relevant and accurate. The letter is easy to read because of the coherent arrangement of information, the logical sequencing of sentences and the use of connectives within paragraphs. A range of vocabulary is attempted and there are some examples of less common words, but errors are quite frequent in noun phrases and spelling. With regard to grammar, there are frequent errors in verb forms and subject/verb agreement, especially in complex structures, but there is a good mix of sentence types.

General Training Writing Example 2 – Task 2

Sample Response 10

Zoos. We Need You or Not.

Last month, I went to the Dublin Zoo with my best friend Jack and his families. I can not remember when was the last time I went to the Zoo and see the animals. anyway it is long time ago. ~~and I remember~~ , that time I was a kid and I was very very happy.

We arrived the Zoo around 11:00 AM, Jack's two children they ~~were~~ so exciting. keep running. keep asking question keep taking photos .... but I did not feel happy any more. I saw the "wild animals" were locked in a small cage. they even didn't move at all. you can not believe they lived in the forest before. I felt sorry for them. I talked with Jack about what I felt, he answered. "Pal, I had the same feeling. if you think you give the ~~food~~ and water to the animals that is enough, no, you wrong, they need freedom, the same as human." Human can fight for their freedom. use their ~~hands~~, guns, even use their lifes But poor animals they want to do it, but ~~compare~~ against with their ~~emery~~ — human. they will never win.

When we left the Zoo around 4:00 PM in the afternoon, We saw a group deers ~~passed~~ crossed the road. I saw them running, I even saw their smelling faces.

On the other hand, Zoos still have some advantages. First, the kids love the Zoos, they can get knowledges the books and DVDs can not give to them, use there as a class to teach them love our world, love our earth. Second, you can save the animals, some animals they nearly disapper from the earth, like panda, we have to protect them, let the number grow up again, and later we can let them back to their ~~really~~ real home.

Trade the animals as your friend, even if they are in the Zoo, I hope in the future, all the animals will free from the Zoo, enjoy their lifes.

Examiner Comments

Band 5

This candidate has chosen to take an unusually personal approach to the topic, so that the basis of the response is an extended narrative of an event. This is not an appropriate format for a task that requires a discursive text. Although the content of the story is relevant, the extent of this personal account detracts from the overall response to the question. Rather than being used just as an illustrative example, the narrative takes over the whole response so that the story of the zoo visit outweighs the general discussion. However, both viewpoints are discussed, albeit too indirectly, and the writer's own opinion comes through clearly. There is some organisation to the response. However, the content is not always arranged coherently, and the paragraphing is not always adequate. The vocabulary used is fairly simple, and there are errors of spelling, word form and word choice. However, the vocabulary resource is just sufficient to achieve the task. Complex structures are attempted but also contain errors.

How Speaking is Assessed

The Speaking test assesses whether candidates can communicate effectively in English.

Speaking performance is assessed by certified examiners who are appointed by the test centre and approved by the British Council or IDP: IELTS Australia.

The examiner rates the candidate's performance throughout the Speaking test, using detailed performance descriptors. These describe speaking performance at the nine IELTS bands according to four different criteria:

Fluency and Coherence
This criterion refers to the ability to talk with normal levels of continuity, rate and effort, and to link ideas and language together to form coherent, connected speech.

Speech rate and speech continuity provide evidence of the fluency criterion.

Logical sequencing of spoken sentences, clear marking of stages in a discussion, narration or argument, and the use of cohesive devices (e.g. connectors, pronouns and conjunctions) within and between sentences provide evidence of the coherence criterion.

Lexical Resource
This criterion refers to the ability to use a range of vocabulary and to express meanings and attitudes with precision.

The variety of words used, the adequacy and appropriacy of the words used, and the ability to overcome vocabulary gaps by using other words provide evidence of the lexical resource criterion.

Grammatical Range and Accuracy
This criterion refers to the ability to use a range of grammatical items accurately and appropriately.

The length and complexity of the spoken sentences, the appropriate use of subordinate clauses, and the range of structures used provide evidence of the grammatical range criterion.

The frequency of grammatical errors and the communicative effect of such errors provide evidence of the grammatical accuracy criterion.

Pronunciation
This criterion refers to the ability to use a range of phonological features consistently and accurately to convey meaning.

The intelligibility of sounds produced, the appropriate use of rhythm, stress and intonation, and the degree of effort required by the listener to understand what is being said provide evidence of the pronunciation criterion.

All criteria have equal weighting.

The public version of the Speaking band descriptors is available on the IELTS website **www.ielts.org**

Sample Candidate Speaking Tests and Examiner Comments

On the DVD included at the back of the booklet, you will find three candidate Speaking tests. Below, you will find examiner comments on each test and the Band Scores given.

The examiner guidelines for assessing candidate performance on the Speaking test are very detailed. There are many different ways a candidate may achieve a particular Band Score. The candidate performances on the DVD should not be regarded as definitive examples of any particular Band Score.

Speaking Test Example 1: French male
Examiner Comments
Band 5

The candidate keeps going, but relies on hesitation, repetition and correction while he searches for language. He uses some cohesive devices but these are fairly basic and are limited in range. His use of vocabulary is adequate for the topics, but his restricted vocabulary and lack of flexibility is evident in the frequent searches for words, the overuse of some words such as 'stressful', and in the frequent inappropriacies in word choice and formation. His grammar contains noticeable and frequent errors in such areas as pronouns, singular/plural forms and verb tenses. He does attempt complex structures but with limited accuracy. His pronunciation is generally easy to understand, although his syllable stress can cause problems, as with 'karate'. His strong French accent and syllable-timed language have an effect on his rhythm and chunking. This candidate is able to express his thoughts on a variety of topics, but the lack of flexibility and number of errors limit him to a Band 5.

Speaking Test Example 2: Turkish female
Examiner Comments
Band 5.5

This candidate keeps going and gives extended responses at reasonable speed, although there is occasional loss of coherence, as at the end of part 2. She uses a range of discourse markers and cohesive devices, although her range is fairly limited. Her range of vocabulary is one of the strong points of the interview: it is sufficient to discuss topics at length and she displays some use of idiomatic language as in the use of phrasal verbs. She does have occasional problems accessing the words she requires, and makes errors in both word choice and word formation. However, she is able to paraphrase, and errors do not interfere with communication. Her grammar is her weakest feature: there is over-dependence on the use of present simple with very variable control over other tenses. There are also incomplete clauses with missing pronouns or auxiliary verbs. Her pronunciation is generally clear and there is some use of stress and intonation to convey meaning. However, her speech is mainly syllable-timed and this leads to a rather mechanical rhythm. The candidate has a good range of vocabulary and speaks with reasonable fluency, but is less effective in the range and accuracy of her grammar. This limits her to a Band 5.5.

Speaking Test Example 3: Syrian female
Examiner Comments
Band 7

The candidate speaks fluently and gives appropriate and extended responses to the questions and tasks. She has a wide and effective use of discourse markers and cohesive devices. There is occasional hesitation or repetition while she searches for language, but this does not affect coherence. She uses a wide range of vocabulary, including some less common and idiomatic items and an effective use of collocation. However, there are some inappropriacies in word choice and formation. Her grammar has a good range of both simple and complex structures. Many of her sentences are error-free, but there are noticeable errors in areas such as articles, prepositions, and occasionally in verb tense. Her pronunciation is clear and easy to follow. She uses both sentence stress and intonation effectively to convey meaning. Her accent is noticeable in the occasional stressing of weak forms and in some faulty syllable stress within words; however, this does not affect intelligibility. This is a high-level candidate with good range of language. The number of errors and variable control limit her rating to a Band 7.

Completing the Answer Sheets

Candidates are required to transfer their answers to an answer sheet for the Listening, Academic Reading and General Training Reading tests. The answer sheet is double-sided – one side for Listening and the other side for Reading. Ten minutes' extra time is allowed for transferring answers at the end of the Listening test. In the Reading test candidates are required to write their answers on the answer sheet during the time allowed for the test. **No extra time is allowed for transfer of the Reading answers.**

An example of a completed Listening answer sheet is given below. Please note the instructions for completing the answer sheet.

Candidates must take care when writing their answers on the answer sheet, as poor spelling and grammar are penalised.

After marking at the test centre, all answer sheets are returned to Cambridge ESOL for analysis.

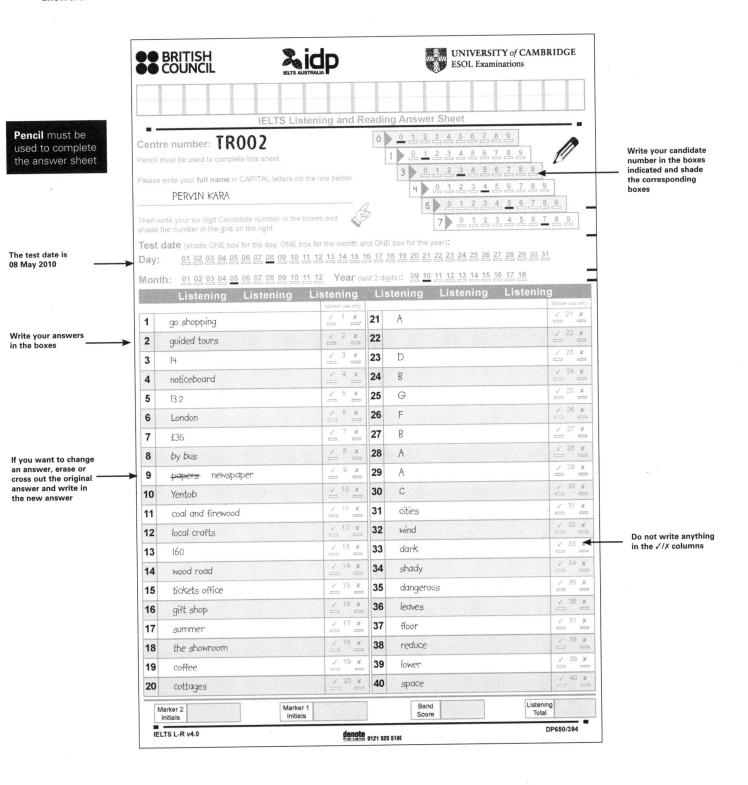

Listening Answer Sheet

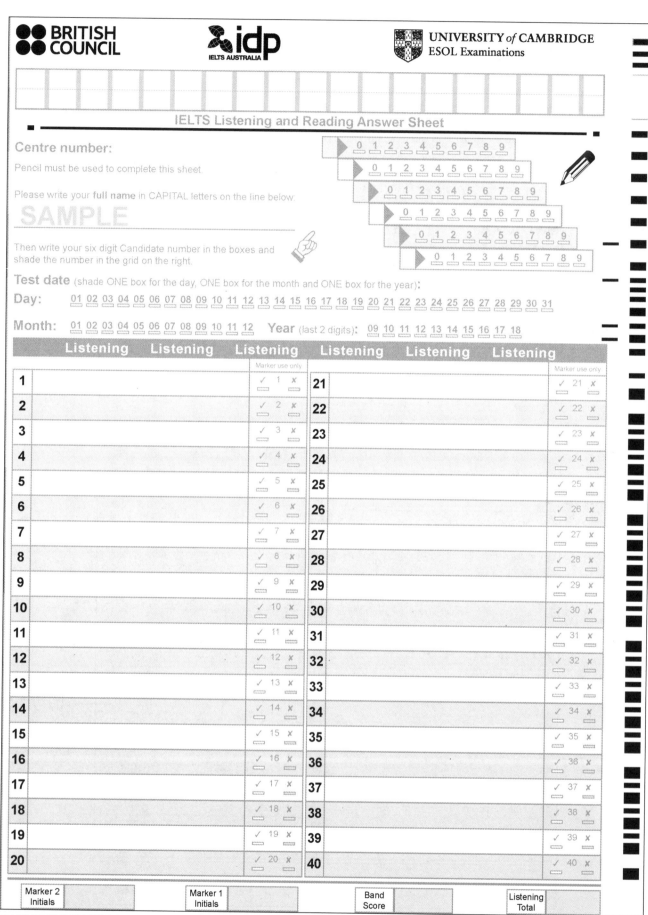

Academic/General Training Reading Answer Sheet

Please write your **full name** in CAPITAL letters on the line below:

SAMPLE

Please write your Candidate number on the line below:

Please write your three digit language code in the boxes and shade the numbers in the grid on the right.

0 1 2 3 4 5 6 7 8 9

0 1 2 3 4 5 6 7 8 9

0 1 2 3 4 5 6 7 8 9

Are you: Female? ⬜   Male? ⬜

Reading   Reading   Reading   Reading   Reading   Reading

Module taken (shade one box):   Academic ⬜   General Training ⬜

	Marker use only			Marker use only
1		**21**		✓ 21 ✗
2	✓ 2 ✗	**22**		✓ 22 ✗
3	✓ 3 ✗	**23**		✓ 23 ✗
4	✓ 4 ✗	**24**		✓ 24 ✗
5	✓ 5 ✗	**25**		✓ 25 ✗
6	✓ 6 ✗	**26**		✓ 26 ✗
7	✓ 7 ✗	**27**		✓ 27 ✗
8	✓ 8 ✗	**28**		✓ 28 ✗
9	✓ 9 ✗	**29**		✓ 29 ✗
10	✓ 10 ✗	**30**		✓ 30 ✗
11	✓ 11 ✗	**31**		✓ 31 ✗
12	✓ 12 ✗	**32**		✓ 32 ✗
13	✓ 13 ✗	**33**		✓ 33 ✗
14	✓ 14 ✗	**34**		✓ 34 ✗
15	✓ 15 ✗	**35**		✓ 35 ✗
16	✓ 16 ✗	**36**		✓ 36 ✗
17	✓ 17 ✗	**37**		✓ 37 ✗
18	✓ 18 ✗	**38**		✓ 38 ✗
19	✓ 19 ✗	**39**		✓ 39 ✗
20	✓ 20 ✗	**40**		✓ 40 ✗

Marker 2 Initials ⬜

Marker 1 Initials ⬜

Band Score ⬜

Reading Total ⬜

Academic/General Training Writing Answer Booklet

INTERNATIONAL ENGLISH LANGUAGE TESTING SYSTEM

UNIVERSITY of CAMBRIDGE
ESOL Examinations

WRITING ANSWER BOOKLET

Candidate Name: ....   Candidate Number: ....

Centre Number: .... Date: ....

Module: ACADEMIC ☐   GENERAL TRAINING ☐   (Tick as appropriate)

TASK 1

_____

_____

_____

_____

_____

_____

_____

_____

_____

_____

EXAMINER'S USE ONLY

EXAMINER 2 NUMBER: ....

CANDIDATE NUMBER: ....   EXAMINER 1 NUMBER: ....

EXAMINER 2 TASK 1	TA		CC		LR		GRA	

UNDERLENGTH		NO OF WORDS		PENALTY	
OFF-TOPIC		MEMORISED		ILLEGIBLE	

EXAMINER 1 TASK 1	TA		CC		LR		GRA	

UNDERLENGTH		NO OF WORDS		PENALTY	
OFF-TOPIC		MEMORISED		ILLEGIBLE	

EXAMINER'S USE ONLY

EXAMINER 2 TASK 2	TR		CC		LR		GRA	

UNDERLENGTH		NO OF WORDS		PENALTY	
OFF-TOPIC		MEMORISED		ILLEGIBLE	

EXAMINER 1 TASK 2	TR		CC		LR		GRA	

UNDERLENGTH		NO OF WORDS		PENALTY	
OFF-TOPIC		MEMORISED		ILLEGIBLE	